The WAY of Agape

UNDERSTANDING GOD'S LOVE

NANCY MISSLER

Leader's Guide

The King's High Way Series ®

Leader's Guide

For

The WAY of Agape

Personal Application Workbook

by

Nancy Missler

The King's *High* Way Ministries

Personal Application Workbook Leader's Guide

for *The Way of Agape*

© Copyright 1995 by Nancy Missler

Published by
The King's *High* Way Ministries
P.O. Box 3111
Coeur d'Alene, ID 83816
www.kingshighway.org
(866)775-5464

ISBN 978-0-9745177-6-6

All Scripture quotations are from the King James Version of the Holy Bible.

PRINTED IN THE UNITED STATES OF AMERICA

The Way of Agape
DVD & Audio Outline
Teaching Starts with Chapter 3

Session 1 - What is God's Love and Why it's so Important (Chapters 3 & 4)

Chapter 3
- What is God's Love
- Four Characteristics of God's Love

Chapter 4
- Why God's Love is So Important
- Jesus is our example

Session 2 - Human Love & How it differs from God's Love, Our Identity & Security & Knowing that God Loves us (Chapters 5-7)

Chapter 5
- Four Attributes of Human Love
- Three Natural Loves

Chapter 6
- Our Identity & Security

Chapter 7
- Knowing God Loves Us
- Can We Prove God Loves US

Session 3 - What does it mean to love God? And, Satan's three Temptations (Chapters 8 & 9)

Chapter 8
- Loving God
- *Agapao* Defined
- To Love (*Agapao*) God means

Chapter 9
- Satan's Three Temptations

Session 4 - We are the Temple of God (Chapter 10)

Chapter 10
- We Are The Temple of God
- Our New Spirit
- Our New Heart
- Our New Willpower
- Spirit Filled Soul
- Spirit Quenched

Session 5 - Loving God with all our Heart & Will (Chapters 11 & 12)

Chapter 11
- What Does it Mean to Love God With All Our Heart
- What is Sin

Chapter 12
- What Does it Mean to Love God With All Our Will
- God Changes Our Feelings
- Two Continual Choices: Emotional Choice or Faith Choice

Session 6 - Loving God with all our Soul (Chapter 13)

Chapter 13
- What is Our Soul
- Healthy Self Image
- Three Areas of Our Soul

Session 7 - Eight Steps to Survival (Chapter 14)

Chapter 14
- Four Essential Attitudes
- Four Mandatory Steps
- "Give it to God"

Session 8 - Loving Others as Ourselves & Loving in our Marriages (Chapters 15 & 16)

Chapter 15
- Love as Jesus Loved
- Practical Things We Can Do to "Love Others"

Chapter 16
How Does "Loving Others as Ourselves" Apply to Our Marriages
- Doesn't Mean Overlooking Sin
- Our Responsibility - God's Responsibility

Table of Contents *

* Please note that all suggested answers have corresponding pages in the textbook where they can be found.

Welcome!

My intention for this Leader's Guide is simply to help you, the leader of the small group, review The Way of Agape materials and to help you stay focused on the suggested answers for the Study Guide questions. There are no "right" answers; these are just suggestions. The suggestion answers are italicized for easy reference. You add your own answers as the Holy Spirit shows you new and wondrous things.

Again, it has been proven over and over that true spiritual growth does <u>not</u> come from simply reading a book or attending a class, but by the personal application of the material to one's life—i.e., by joining small group discussions, sharing the principles with friends and, of course, by actually living it at home.

Please encourage the participants to try to make <u>all</u> the classes as each one builds upon the material we have learned from the previous class.

I would suggest keeping the discussion group as small as possible. If you have 50 participants, 10 groups of 5 each is ideal; you might also have 5 groups of 10 each. I would not suggest discussion groups larger than 15. It's helpful to have an assistant leader in case you have to miss one or two times yourself. Prayer is the key to everything.

I will be praying that God will be with you, teaching and speaking to you mightily and giving you a hunger and thirst to reach out to your community in His Way of Love.

I love you.

Agape,

Nan

If you have any questions regarding this study, please don't hesitate to call

The King's High Way Ministries @ 1 866 775 5464 or 208 772 6976

Group Leader's Overview

Role of the Discussion Leader

Your role as a leader is simply to stimulate discussion by asking the appropriate questions and encouraging people to respond.

Your leadership is a gift to the other members of the group. Keep in mind that they, too, share responsibility for the group. If you are nervous, realize you are not the first to feel this way. Many Biblical leaders—Moses, Joshua, and even Paul—felt nervous and inadequate to lead others.

Leader Objectives

The following are suggested objectives to help you become an effective leader:

- To guide the discussion, to clarify understanding, and to keep the group focused on the lesson.

- To steer the group into a meaningful exchange among themselves.

- To help the participants learn from each other.

- To keep the group discussion focused on the key points found in the Scriptural Reference Outlines at the end of each chapter.

- To be a neutral person, leading the discussion back to Scripture and the key points if it wanders.

- To assist the group in finding practical applications for the principles discussed. To encourage each person to participate in the group discussion.

- To make the discussion group a nonthreatening place for all to share their ideas.

- To have a positive attitude and to provide encouragement to the group.

- To guide, rather than dominate, the discussion.

Preparing to Lead

First of all, it's critical that you, the leader of the discussion group, be a cleansed vessel filled with God's Love and Wisdom—a "living example" of God's Way of Agape. This message must first be applied to your own life. Otherwise, you will not be genuinely prepared to lead others. You must have a working knowledge of the Way of Agape principles, so you can share what God has done in your own life. You cannot "give out" something you have never "experienced" for yourself.

Only by being real and transparent yourself, sharing your own failures as well as your victories, will genuineness ever be brought into the discussion. It's important to remember that *you don't have to be "perfect" in order to guide a discussion, you simply must be an open vessel pointing others to the only One who is perfect—and that's J1esus.*

Paramount to any Bible study is prayer. Be sure to pray for the group before and after each study and do much private prayer during the discussion itself. Pray for each member of the group during the week, always remembering that prayer is the only thing that unleashes the power of God to work in all our lives.

Read the assigned chapter in <u>The Way of Agape</u> textbook. Answer each question in the corresponding chapter in the workbook. Meditate and reflect upon each passage of Scripture as you formulate your answers.

Familiarize yourself with the <u>Scriptural Reference Outlines</u> at the end of each chapter in the textbook. These will help you understand the important points to make in the discussion and provide more information about the questions.

As a leader, you must be a sensitive listener, not only to the members of the group but also to the Holy Spirit. As you ask the appropriate questions, allow the Holy Spirit to direct your responses and give you discernment as to who needs a special touch (a hug, an encouragement, time afterwards, etc.).

Remember, as the leader of the discussion, you are simply a channel God is using to stimulate and guide the conversation—the Holy Spirit is always the teacher. Do <u>not</u> do all the talking, but involve every member of the group, always seeing that the sharing is edifying and pointed towards Jesus.

Leading the Study

Always begin the study on time. If everyone realizes that you begin on time, the members of the group will make a greater effort to be there on time—they won't want to miss anything.

At the beginning of your first meeting, you might share that these studies are designed to be discussions, not lectures. Encourage everyone to participate.

The discussion questions in the workbook are designed to be used just as they are written. If you wish, you may read each one aloud to the group. Or you may prefer to express them in your own words. However, unnecessary rewording of the questions is not recommended.

Don't be afraid of silence. People in the group need time to think before responding.

Try to avoid answering your own questions. If necessary, keep rephrasing a question until it is clearly understood. If the group thinks you will always answer for them, they will keep silent.

Encourage more than one answer to each question. You might ask, "What do the rest of you think?" or "Anyone else?" Allow several people to respond.

Never reject an answer. Be as affirming as possible. If a person's answer is clearly wrong, you might ask, "What lead you to that conclusion?" or let the group handle the problem by asking them what they think about the question.

Avoid going off on tangents. If people wander off course, gently bring them back to the question at hand.

Try to end on time. This is often difficult to do, but if you control the pace of the discussion by not spending too much time on some questions, you should be able to finish at the appropriate time. A discussion group of about 45 minutes to an hour is perfect.

Additional Suggestions for Leaders

Besides being that open and cleansed vessel and constantly praying, there are several other *skills* that you, as the leader of the discussion, should pray about developing:

Pray for and develop good *communication skills*. Communication will not only be your words, but also your "body language." Even though someone might share something shocking in the discussion, be careful not to offend the participant by your response. Acknowledge the person, yet all the while asking God for *His* response to what they have just shared. Be confident that God will give you the Love you need and also the Wisdom you need to respond "wisely in Love."

Try to really understand what the participant is sharing. If necessary, repeat what you think he/she is saying. For example, you might ask: "Is this what you are saying...?" or, "You mean...?"

Another very important asset for you, as the leader of the group, to acquire is to be a *good listener*. Everyone is desperate for someone to listen to them, especially when they are going through critical emotional issues. Whenever someone is talking, give them your undivided attention. Your eyes should be on the person sharing and you should try to acknowledge them as much as you can (again, always praying silently to God for <u>His</u> response).

Another vital skill to develop is *to be an encourager*. Set an example for your group by encouraging the members continually. Without encouragement, your sharing times will be nothing more than answering homework questions at school. (You might even suggest that the following week, each of the members of the group phone and encourage someone else in the group.)

One of the most difficult tasks that you will face *is how to keep one person from dominating* the group. You need to allow each person in the group an opportunity to share, but you must prevent any *one* person from doing all the talking (including yourself). One member of the group who continually dominates the discussion can derail and quench an otherwise anointed sharing time. You mustn't rush the person speaking, giving the Holy Spirit ample time to minister and guide the discussion, but at the same time you are responsible to keep the discussion on target and to accomplish all that needs to be done.

A few suggestions to prevent one person from dominating the discussion:

- You might interrupt the particular person speaking and restate what you have just heard him/her say.

- You might repeat the question you previously asked the group. The dominating person might be startled at first by the interruption, but should respond by answering the second question more directly.

- If this does not work, then you should ask the participant to please let the other group members share their views also.

Another invaluable skill for you, as the leader of the discussion, is knowing how to *involve all the members* of the group in the discussion. Discussion groups are not for lecturing—each individual must be encouraged to interact. Ideally, everyone should have an opportunity to share. Ask open-ended questions to specific individuals, especially ones that are reluctant to volunteer anything themselves.

Again, it's important not to criticize, make fun of, or put anyone down. Remember, be an encourager. Learn how to correct a group member's answer in a positive way and then, as tactfully as you can, go on to the next person.

Helpful Hints for Leaders

Always open the discussion with prayer and close the session with prayer. Pray that God will help each of you to apply the Biblical principles daily.

Start out the first session by sharing a little about yourself. How has the Way of Agape affected or changed your life? Go around the circle and have each member share five minutes about him/her- self.

In the succeeding meetings, begin each session by asking:

- "Which key points stood out to you during this session?"

- "Which points challenged you or encouraged you?"

- "Could any of you relate to some of the situations or struggles that were shared in this chapter?"

- "Are any of you experiencing similar situations?"

- "In what areas of your life might you be able to apply this teaching?"

Suggest that each member of the group during the week write down any questions they may have while reading the textbook, listening to the tapes, or watching the video, so they can talk about them during the group discussion.

Lean heavily on the Scriptural Reference Outlines at the end of each chapter for the *key points* to emphasize.

Reproduce **Charts 1-6** in Chapter Ten of The Way of Agape textbook and post them in each of the appropriate sessions, so the group can constantly refer to them.

Finally, stress complete confidentiality. Set an example for the group by being the first to be trustworthy.

Chapter 1: Introduction
The Flight of the Phoenix
No DVD Teaching

The Way of Agape teaches you about a new way of loving. It's a way of loving that is totally opposite from the way the world teaches and is probably totally opposite from the way you have been used to, even as a Christian.

The Way of Agape is not just for women, nor is it just for married people. Wherever there is a relationship, God's Way of Agape is needed. It really doesn't matter if you have been a Christian seven months, seven years, or 77 years. It doesn't matter how many Scriptures you know, how many prayers you say, how many Bible studies you lead, or even how many books you write; it's still a moment-by-moment choice to "love God" and to lay your life down to Him so that His Love can be poured forth through you.

Purpose of the Study Guide

True spiritual growth comes not from simply reading a book or attending a Bible study, but by the personal application of the material to your life.

You will gain the maximum benefit from these questions by reading the corresponding chapter. You will quickly see how specific Scriptures apply to your own situation. You will receive deeper insights into God's character and His great Love for you. You will also begin to understand your own natural reactions a little more clearly and, at the same time, learn an alternative way of dealing with them.

It is our desire to help you intimately experience God's Love, Wisdom, and Power in your daily life so you can have that "abundant life" He promises.

How To Use This Study Guide

These questions correspond to each chapter in this textbook.

The study guide questions are divided into three categories: **Group Discussion Questions**, Personal Questions, and Continue at Home Questions.

- If you will be using this study for personal Bible study, it is suggested that you do all the study guide questions (Personal, Group, and Continue at Home).

- If this study is to be used by small discussion groups, it is suggested that the leader of the group use the Group Discussion Questions and whatever Personal Questions are applicable. Continue at Home projects can be used during the week.

- Finally, if this study is to be used for a large, corporate group (where small discussion groups are not feasible), it is suggested that the appropriate questions be selected by the leadership and used for individual home study.

Personal Bible Study

Critical to any Bible study, whether it be personal or corporate, is prayer. Pray and ask God to search your heart and reveal anything that might hinder you from hearing Him. Then cleanse your heart of these things, so you can receive all that He has for you.

Along with your Bible, it is often helpful to have the following: a Bible Dictionary to look up any unfamiliar words, names and places; and a concordance.

Read the appropriate chapter in the textbook. You must understand the principles and concepts of The Way of Agape textbook before you can really answer the questions properly and apply the principles to your life.

Look up all the Scriptures listed under each question. Meditate upon each one. It's the Word of God that will change your life, not a textbook or a class. Write out on 3x5 cards the Scriptures that particularly minister to you. Look up the important words in the original Hebrew or Greek, using your Strong's Concordance. Then you can be sure you are getting the real meaning of each word. So often the English translation in the Bible is far from what the original word meant.

Write out your answers in a separate notebook.

It's important to keep a personal journal. Write down all your experiences with God. Note the promises He gives you from Scripture, as well as the experiences He allows in your life. Express your real feelings and emotions about these things—no one should ever see your journal but you. Most importantly, write down the things that you give over to God as you cleanse your heart each day.

What a blessing and an encouragement this journal will be when you read it later on. In those times when you are going through a "valley," your entries in the journal will remind you of all that God has done for you and of His complete faithfulness to perform His promises. Your journal will give you the encouragement and the hope to make the same faith choices again.

Group Bible Study

Learning takes place through the understanding and sharing of Biblical principles with intimate friends, such as in a small discussion group. A discussion group of about eight to ten people is ideal, and each of these groups should have a leader to guide the sharing.

The first thing to do in all Bible studies is to pray. Prayer is what changes things—our hearts, our attitude, our situation, other people, etc. Pray continually. Look up all the Scriptures listed under each question. Meditate upon each one. It's the Word of God that will change your life, not a textbook or a class.

Be willing to join in the discussions. If you have completed the questions and have some understanding of the chapter, you will feel comfortable in sharing. The leader of the group is not there to lecture, but to encourage others to share what they have learned.

Have your answers applicable to the chapter in discussion. Keep the discussion centered upon the principles presented in The Way of Agape textbook, rather than on what you have "heard" others say or on what you have "read" elsewhere. Keep focused.

Be sensitive to the other members of the group. Listen when they speak and be encouraging to them. This will prompt more people to share.

Do not dominate the discussion. Participate, but remember that others need to have equal time.

If you are a discussion leader, suggested answers, additional suggestions, and helpful ideas are in The Way of Agape Leader's Guide. Also, see the "Role of the Discussion Leader" section at the end of this study guide.

Above all, pray for God's guidance and grace to love Him as He desires and be that open vessel to pass along His Love.

Chapter 2: Up in Flames
No DVD Teaching

God's Way of Agape is

• Learning what God's Love is and that God loves us with this same kind of Love.

• Learning what it means to love God in return.

• Learning what it means to love others as ourselves.

Purpose of being a Christian

• To be emptied of self-life and filled with His Life so others might see Jesus in us.

• To be genuine witnesses of Christ—reflecting His Image.

Why does God allow trials?

• To fulfill His purpose in us (see above).

• He loves us and wants us healed—freed from Satan's strongholds.

• He wants us to experience His abundant Life.

• He wants us conformed into His Image.

Maturity in Christ is simply

• Learning how, moment by moment, to love God and then others.

• Recognizing our self-life and making the appropriate faith choices to give it all over to God.

• Staying an open and cleansed vessel prepared for what God has next.

Group Discussion Questions

1. What is our *purpose* as Christians? (Romans 8:29; Ephesians 3:17-19; 1 Timothy 1:5; Ephesians 5:1-2; John 13:34-35; 1 John 4:16-17) How are we to fulfill this purpose? (Matthew 22:37-40; Mark 8:35; 1 John 3:16; 4:12)

    Our purpose as Christians is to be conformed into the Image of Christ; to be filled with the fullness of God (His Life); to have His Love flowing from our hearts; to be a sweet-smelling savour; and to love one another so all will know we are Christians.

    We fulfill this purpose by learning to love God; yielding our lives to Him; and, letting His Love flow through us.
    (Pages 27, 30-31, 33)

2. Identify the specific actions and attitudes laid down by our Lord in Luke 14:25-35 for anyone who would be His disciple.

    The attitude that Jesus desires for all of us is to be willing to yield and relinquish everything to Him, to be willing to carry our own cross and come after Him; to be willing to forsake all that we have in order to follow Him; and to be willing to love, even if our circumstances and the other person never change.

    (Page 31)

3. How would you describe "abundant Life?" (John 10:10)

    Abundant Life is simply God Life (His Supernatural Love, Wisdom, and Power) freely flowing through us and becoming our life in our souls.

    (Page 31)

4. Why do you think God allows trials in our lives? (Deuteronomy 30:19-20; 13:3-4; Psalm 119:67; John 15:2)

    God allows trials in our lives in order to force us to choose. God wants us to choose to love Him by obeying His voice and by cleaving unto Him (for He is our Life). He tests us to see if we do, indeed, love Him with all our heart and soul—to see if we will keep His commands and serve Him. Before our trials, we often go astray because we follow our own ways. God purges us through our trials so that we might learn His ways and, thus, bear more fruit.

    (Page 33)

5. 2 Corinthians 4:10 talks about the "dying of Jesus." Share what this means to you. What is the "life of Jesus" spoken about here?

    The "dying of Jesus" means the death of self; it means learning to relinquish, set aside, and yield all our own thoughts, emotions, and desires that are contrary to Jesus'. (John 12:25)

    The "Life of Jesus" means His Love, His Wisdom and His Power (and all the fruits of the Spirit) coming forth from our lives. This is the Abundant Life we are all seeking. (1 Corinthians 13, Galatians 5:22)

    (Pages 27, 31, 33)

6. Review in detail the three steps of God's *Way of Agape*. (Matthew 22:37-40; John 12:24-25; 2 Corinthians 4:10-12; Matthew 16:24)

    The Way of Agape is:

    1) Learning what God's Love is and that He loves us with this same kind of unconditional Love.

    2) Learning what it means to love God.

    3) And finally, learning what it means to love others.

The Way of Agape is important because it's the only way others will see Jesus in us; the only way to pass along His Love; and the only way to live without hypocrisy.

(Pages 32-33, 37-38)

7.   1 John 3:14 says that if we are not loving with God's Love, then we are dying. What does this mean to you?

This Scripture says that he who doesn't love (allow God's Love to flow through him) doesn't really "know" God and he has not passed from death unto Life. If we don't love, this Scripture says we are still abiding in death.

I believe this also applies to Christians who refuse to allow God's Love to flow through them.

(Pages 19-24)

Personal Questions

1.   Have you or are you experiencing any situations or struggles similar to those that were shared in this chapter? If so, what situations?

Ask questions like:

- Do any of you have something you want to share?

- What is God trying to teach you through this trial?

- Did your attitude change through this trial?

- Can you recall any situations where you had to confront someone in God's Love?

- What were the results?

- Have you ever held in justified feelings?

- What happened?

2.   READ Mark 10:17-22. Why do you think the rich young ruler could not give up his possessions? Can you name anything that would be difficult for you to give up now?

This Scripture says the rich young ruler had many possessions and therefore, couldn't put Jesus first in his life. It's the same with us. Often our husbands, children, jobs, careers, houses, and other things become more important than God in our own lives.

3.   Summarize why it is so important to spend time alone with the Lord every day in order to live *The Way of Agape*?

Time alone with the Lord is where we bring our burdens to Him. This is where we can make the choice to cleanse ourselves, (confess, repent, and give all to Him). This is where we are refilled with His Spirit and are thus prepared for whatever He brings next into our lives.

4.   How would you describe your own quiet time this week? List the things that seem
      to interfere.

      Stress the importance of "renewal" and cleansing in our quiet times. Ask them to
      share what has helped them to do this.

5.   1 John 4:17 says: "... as He is, so are we in this world." Share what this means to
      you.

      Go around the circle and get their various answers. To me it means living His Life,
      sharing His Love (He is Love), and that's what we are to be in this world.

Continue at Home

1.   Write on a note card any Scriptures that particularly ministered to you in this
      chapter. Use them to help you apply these principles. Memorize them. Carry them
      with you or post them where you can see them as a reminder.

      Suggest to the group to categorize scriptures: on comfort, love, wisdom,
      forgiveness, etc.

2.   This week, talk to God about improving the quality of your daily quiet time.
      Schedule a specific time with Him. Listen to worship music that will draw you
      closer to Jesus. Write out some of your prayers. Use a daily reading guide to help
      you be consistent with your Bible reading. Be accountable to someone for this
      time.

3.   Ask God to show you the areas that you are still not willing to lay down to Him.
      (You might not even be aware of them.)

      An attitude of "willingness to love" is critical; ask God to show you where you are
      lacking.

4.   Begin a journal. Write down all the experiences God allows in your life this week
      that you need to "deal" with—situations you didn't handle properly or attitudes you
      developed that were not godly. Describe your own thoughts and emotions about
      the situation. *Confess* any of your thoughts or emotions that are not of faith and
      repent of them—choose to turn around from following them. *Give those negative
      thoughts and emotions to God*, and then *read His Word*. Ask Him to replace those
      negative things with His truth.

MEMORIZE:
John 12:24-25
2 Corinthians 4:10-12
Matthew 16:24

Chapter 3: What is God's Love?
Session 1 – DVD 1 - 56 minutes

What is God's Love?

- Agape is the Greek word for God's Love.

- God is Love (Agape).

- Agape is a pure, supernatural, and unconditional Love.

- Definition of Agape (1 Corinthians 13:4-8).

- Agape is God Himself loving through us.

Agape is not a natural love, but a supernatural Love

- Agape is not dependent upon our human understanding, our human emotions, or our human desires.

- Agape is not dependent upon others' responses.

- Agape is not dependent upon our circumstances.

- It's only dependent upon God and His faithfulness.

Four characteristics of God's Love

- It's unconditional—it loves no matter what.

- It's one-sided—it doesn't have to be returned to be kept alive.

- It's freeing—it not only frees the lover from expectations, but it also frees the one being loved to respond from his heart.

- It's other-centered—it always puts the others' interests above its own.

Other significant attributes of Agape

- It causes "contrary to normal" reactions from those being loved.

- It exposes the sin of the one being loved.

- It never fails.

- It includes unconditional forgiveness.

Chesed is the Old Testament word for Love

- It can be a long-suffering Love.

- It can be a discipline Love.

In order to love with God's Love, we must:

- Make faith choices (The Key).

- Set self aside and become a cleansed vessel. God then loves His Love through us.

Group Discussion Questions

1.   Define God's Love in your own words. List further qualities of God's Love found in the following passages: 1 Corinthians 13:1-8; 1 John 4:7-8, 16b; Galatians 5:22-24.

     "God is Love."

     God's Love is: patient, kind, not jealous, not proud but humble, not irritable, doesn't hold grudges, forgives and doesn't notice others' sins towards them, is always loyal, always thinks and expects the best of others, and defends others. God's Love never stops coming. God's Love is joy, peace, long-suffering, gentleness, goodness, faith, meekness, and temperance.

     (Pages 42-43, 47-48, 51-52, 55)

2.   Name four other *characteristics* of God's Love spoken about in Chapter 3. (Luke 6:27-37; 2 Corinthians 3:17; 1 Corinthians 13:4-8)

     Expand on these passages.

     Four characteristics of God's Love:

     1)   It's <u>unconditional</u> because it loves no matter what.

     2)   It's <u>one-sided</u> because it doesn't have to be returned in order to be kept alive. It's initiating, unilateral Love.

     3)   It's <u>freeing</u> because it frees the person loving from expectations, and it frees the lover to respond from the heart. It's unconditional acceptance.

     4)   It's <u>other-centered</u> because it always puts others' interests first. Other attributes of God's Love:

          - God's Love exposes sin.

          - God's Love is a gift with no strings attached.

          - God's Love is unconditional forgiveness.

     (Pages 43-45, 47-48, 55)

     See also supplemental notes (page 339) for more attributes.

3.   Are we able, in our own power, to produce this kind of Love? Why or why not?

(Romans 7:18; 1 John 4:16; John 15:5; 1 Corinthians 13:8)

Scripture tells us that in our flesh "dwells no good thing." Only if we dwell in God and He in us, will we be able to produce this kind of Love. Agape, therefore, is not automatic—even for Christians. All that is required of us to produce this kind of Love in our lives is our willingness to be a cleansed vessel and to let God love His Love through us.

(Pages 46-47, 52)

4. Explain the difference between loving with God's Love and loving with human, natural love. (1 Corinthians 13:1-8; Luke 6:27-37; Galatians 5:22-24)

When we love with human love, our love will be based upon how we feel and what we think, upon how the other person responds and upon our circumstances. Thus, human love is easily quenched by hurts, fears and other "justified" negative feelings.

God's Love is unconditional and based only upon God. He is always faithful to love that other person no matter how we feel, how they respond or what our circumstances are. God will love through us if we are simply an "open vessel." Our only responsibility is to choose to be yielded to God; He then changes our feelings to match those choices.

(Pages 46-48, 51)

5. Describe the only requirement for having God's Love. (John 3:3-5; 17:26; Romans 5:5)

The only requirement for having God's Love is having Jesus and His Love in our hearts. Being born again, we already have God's Life in our hearts (His Love, Wisdom and Power).

(Pages 41-42)

6. Define what further steps are required for us to love others with God's Love. (1 John 3:16; Matthew 16:24; 2 Corinthians 4:10-11)

Further steps required for us to love others are:

1) Our willingness to be an open and cleansed vessel.

2) Our willingness to change first, so God can love His Love through us.

3) Our willingness to make faith choices to allow God to use us.

4) Our willingness to love even if our situations never change.

The KEY is: Learning how to get rid of all the negative things in us that quench God's Love so we can remain cleansed.

(Pages 46-47, 52)

7. 1 Corinthians 13:8 says that God's Love never fails. What does this mean to you?

(Jeremiah 31:3; Psalm 89:33; 103:17)

"God's Love never fails" means that God's Love will never stop coming; it means that it never ceases to flow. Now, we might quench God's Love in our lives by our emotional choices, but His Love will continue to always flow into our hearts.

God's Love is eternal, everlasting and never-ending. So, even if the person we are loving runs from God's Love, that Love will never stop flowing to him.

(Pages 45, 51-52)

8.   Summarize the four *attributes* of God's Love that make it totally unique from any kind of human love. (See Supplemental Notes in Textbook.) Describe each attribute. (Ephesians 1:4-5; John 15:16; Jeremiah 31:3; Isaiah 63:9; Hosea 2:19-20; Deuteronomy 7:9)

The four attributes of God's Love that make it totally unique are:

1)   God's Love is *electing Love*, which means it chooses or selects whom it will love.

2)   God's Love is *initiating Love*, which is a Love that takes the first step. It begins the loving process; it's one-sided Love.

3)   God's Love is *identifying Love*, which means it identifies with the one being loved.

4)   And lastly, God's Love is *faithful and maintaining Love*, which means it loves no matter what the object of that Love is doing. It unconditionally maintains an open relationship.

(Pages 339-341)

9.   What are the two sides of God's Love (called in the Hebrew, *chesed*)? (Psalm 103:4; Job 37:13; Romans 11:22)

Chesed Love, God's Love in the Old Testament, has two sides to it: one side is a long-suffering and merciful Love; the other side is a strict, firm and disciplined Love. Only God, by His Wisdom, can show us how to love "wisely" in each situation.

(Pages 45-46 and Chapter 16, pages 297-298)

10.   Explain the difference between "taking a stand in God's Love" and "confronting" someone on your own. Can you give an example?

"Taking a stand in God's Love" and "confronting someone" on our own power and ability are two totally different ways of handling a situation. Taking a stand in God's Love means you are a cleansed vessel (all your own hurts and emotions have been yielded and given to God) and God's Love is free to flow from your heart out to that other person.

Confronting someone usually occurs in the heat of an argument when one is full of anger and hurt (i.e., a dirty vessel) thus, the life that comes forth is not God's, but their own self-life.

(Pages 44-45, 56)

11. Before we "take a stand" in God's Love, what are some of the critical things *we* must remember to do? (Matthew 16:24)

Before we can take a stand in God's Love, we must first become a cleansed vessel: by confessing our own sin, repenting of it and giving it over to God.

(Pages 26-27, 56 and Chapter 14)

12. God's Love often prompts a response from the one being loved. What are some responses you have noted? (Ephesians 5:13; Romans 2:4b; Jeremiah 31:3b)

Refer to the story, "A Father's Confrontation." God softened the Pastor's heart so that his wife could share from her own heart. The Pastor eventually changed his mind about confronting his daughter in anger. He and his wife then "took a stand in God's Love." They continually kept the emphasis on themselves and didn't accuse their daughter. The daughter felt her parent's genuine

Love which then gave her the freedom to respond from her heart. Thus, the Holy Spirit was able to convict her of her own sin. She repented of it and they all were reconciled.

(Pages 44-45)

Personal Questions

1. At this point, are you willing to lay down every facet of your life so that God can love others through you? If not, what areas are you still struggling with? (1 John 4:7-8, 12, 20)

Ask this of each person. Can each of you say this in your own heart? Any discussion?

2. What are some of your own negative thoughts and emotions that tend to block and prevent God's Love from flowing through you? What determines whether or not these things become sin in your life?

The point at which the negative thoughts and emotions become sin, is when we choose to hold on to them, mull them over in our minds, or bury them. Remember, the first, original negative thought is not sin, it's what we choose to do with that thought that determines if it becomes sin or not.

(Pages 46-47)

3. Can you give an example of a situation where you need to "take a stand in God's Love," but are having difficulty doing so?

Discussion , share.

4.   Think of a situation where you *were able* to love with God's Love regardless of your feelings, the circumstances, or others' responses. Describe it.

      Discussion, share.

5.   Is there an area in your life right now where you can apply this teaching?

      Are there spouses, friends, parents, relatives, houses, neighbors, coworkers, etc. in your life that you need to love with God's Love? Is there anyone you are unable to love?

Continue at Home

1.   Write on a note card any Scriptures that particularly ministered to you in this chapter and use them to help you apply these principles. Memorize them.

2.   Read over the Agape Scriptures in the Supplemental Notes section at the back of The Way of Agape textbook. Write on 3x5 cards the Scriptures that particularly help you and memorize them.

3.   Spend quiet time this week recommitting every area of your life to God.

4.   This week, pray and ask God to make you aware of your own negative and self-centered thoughts and feelings. In your journal, write down what God shows you. Choose to relinquish those thoughts to God. Confess you have "owned" (kept) them. Give those thoughts to God and then replace them with a few of your favorite Scriptures.

5.   Ask God to fill you with His Love and allow that Love to be the motivation for all your choices each day.

READ:	MEMORIZE:
1 Corinthians 13	1 John 3:16
1 John 4	Galatians 5:22-24
Hosea 1-3	John 17:26

Chapter 4: Why Is God's Love So Important?
Session 1 DVD 1 - 16 minutes

God's Love is important because:

- God is Love!

It's the whole meaning and purpose of our Christian walk

- To love God and then to love others.

- Agape is the "goal of our instruction."

- Without Love, we will be empty of meaning.

- If we don't learn to love and be loved, we will have wasted our lives.

- Love and identity are synonymous.

- Love must be the central issue of our lives.

It's the only way others will know we are Christians

- We are extensions of God's Love.

- Others will know (see) Jesus by His Love in us.

It proves we are abiding in God

- Staying in His Love means remaining in His Presence.

- John 15 talks about resting in His Love (carrying fruit from one place to another).

By it we are filled with the fullness of God

- Setting aside our lives—being filled with His Life.

- Experiencing His Life flowing through us.

It is the perfect bond of union—between God and me and others and me

- God's Love initiates a relationship.

- God's Love maintains a relationship.

- God's Love reconciles a relationship.

- God's Love enables us to unconditionally forgive what others have done to us.

It's proof that we do, indeed, love Jesus

- We have reached our goal: the fulfillment of God's purpose.

Group Discussion Questions

1. In your own words summarize the reasons why God's Love is so important. (1 John 4:7-8; 1 Corinthians 13:2; 1 Timothy 1:5: John 13:34-35; Colossians 3:14)

    God's Love is important because:

    1) God is Love.

    2) It's the whole meaning and purpose of our lives—to love God and to love others.

    3) Others will know we are Christians when we love with His Love and when we're extensions of His Love.

    4) Having God's Love proves we are abiding in God. Staying in His Love is carrying His fruit from one place to another.

    5) Having God's Love means we are filled with the fullness of God: God's Life.

    6) God's Love is the perfect bond of union which maintains, unites and reconciles our fellow- ship with each other.

    7) God's Love is proof we love God and have laid down our lives to Him.

        (Pages 57-58, 60-63, 65)

2. Why do you think having and passing on God's Love should be the central issue of our lives? (1 Corinthians 13:1-3; Galatians 5:14; 1 John 3:14)

    Love is the reason we were created in the first place and if we don't learn to be loved and to love in the way God desires, we will have wasted our lives. Scripture says that without His Love, we are nothing. The entire Bible is fulfilled in one word, "Love."

    (Pages 57, 63, 65)

3. Galatians 5:14 tells us that God's Love is the "fulfillment of the law" (Galatians 5:14). What does this mean to you?

    God's Love flowing through us is the proof that we have reached "the goal of our instruction" (1 Timothy 1:5). His Love is the fulfillment of all of God's purposes in us. Again, the whole Bible is summed up in the word Love (Matthew 22:40).

    Having God's Love flowing through us is proof that we love God and others (Matthew 22:36-40).

    (Pages 60-61)

4. The Bible says having God's Love is the only way others will know we are Christians. (John 13:35) Why do you think this is so? Don't all Christians have God's Love showing through them?

    Others will know by hearing our words and seeing our actions that we do, indeed, belong to God. The whole purpose of Bible reading is to make us more loving, not more scholarly. Only Jesus' Love flowing through us (not our own human love) will cause others to know we belong to God.

    (Pages 58-61, 63)

5. John 15 tells us that having God's Love is proof we are abiding in Him. How is this so?

    Abiding in God means staying in His Love & resting in His Love. It means staying open vessels, carrying His fruit from one location to another. Having His Love (His fruit) is, therefore, proof we are indeed, abiding in Him. God's Love is like the barometer.

    (Page 60)

6. Explain what 1 Peter 4:8 means when it says God's Love "covers a multitude of sins."

    "To cover" means to hide or conceal. When we choose to become that open vessel and love with God's Love, we can tear up that long list of justified hurts (we give them, instead, to God) and then the other person's sins are hidden and concealed in God.

    (Pages 48, 52, 67)

Personal Questions

1. Is there an area in your life right now where you can apply this teaching?

    Open discussion. Ask questions like:

    • Is having and passing on God's Love the whole meaning and purpose of your life?

    • Is there anything else in your life that has taken the place of and become more important than God and His Love (your spouse, children, friends, career, house)? (Page 57)

2. Have you or are you now experiencing any situations or struggles similar to those that were shared in this teaching? If so, explain.

    Ask questions like:

    • Have you seen that emptiness and un-fulfillment in others' lives (i.e., family, friends)?

    • How about your own?

3.   Does *loving with God's Love* have that first place in your life right now? (1 Peter 4:8) If not, why not?

Scripture says above everything else, we are to have fervent Agape Love for others. Do you?

4.   Can others tell that you are a Christian by your Love? (1 John 4:8,12,20) How about your husband, your wife, or your family?

This is the hardest test. Remember the Pastor's family in Chapter 3? Everyone thought he was a wonderful Pastor, but his wife knew his weak areas and the areas in which he had no love. How about you? Do your children see Jesus in you? You can't say to them "be a Christian" and yet not live it yourself!

5.   Ephesians 3:19 tells us we are to be "filled with all the fullness of God." Have you ever experienced this? Share examples.

Filled with the fullness of God means to be filled with His Life: His Love, Wisdom and Power. Do you experience this? Discussion.

Note examples in Chapter 3, "A Father's Confrontation," and also, "Justified Wrongs."

Continue at Home

1.   Write on a note card the Scriptures that particularly ministered to you in this chapter. Use them to help you apply these principles. Memorize them this week.

2.   This week ask God to show you personally why His Love is so important to have and to pass on. In your journal, write the things God shows you. Be prepared to share. In your journal, write the things God shows you. Be prepared to share.

READ: MEMORIZE:
1 John 4   1 Peter 4:8
1 Corinthians 13:1-3   1 John 4:7-8, 12, 16-17
John 15   1 Timothy 1:5
Ephesians 3   John 13:34-35

Chapter 5: God's Love vs. Natural Love
DVD -1 Session 2 - 36 minutes

Human love

- Is totally opposite from God's Love.

- Is a love everyone has—but not everyone has God's Love.

- Is a "need love," trying to fulfill its own desires, whereas God's Love is a "gift of Love."

- Must be returned in order to be kept alive.

- Seeks good of itself and not the other person.

- Is always conditional and reciprocal.

- Will always fail and continue to let us down, unless it is built on God's Love as a foundation.

Four attributes of human love

- It's a conditional love—it depends on what we think, feel and desire, our circumstances and others' reactions.

- It's a two-sided love—it says "I'll love you if you love me."

- It's a bondage love—the lover is wrapped up in his own expectations and the person being loved is not free to respond from his heart.

- It's a self-centered love—it hopes that the love given will be returned.

Three human loves

- Storge— our natural, emotional love: Our natural affection love.

    An instinctive love, like the love of a parent for a child.

    Has a desperate need to control—fear of losing other's love

- Eros— our natural, sexual love:

    Our "falling in love," love.

    Has an intoxicating effect.

    Lifts us above our problems.

    Momentarily fills our emptiness.

    Distorts person's self-examination.

- Phileo— anything we have a strong attachment to:

    It's based on a similarity of outlook.

    A mutual attraction love.

    A friendship love—a companionship love.

Problems occur because

- Of confusion between human loves and God's Love—this causes us to get off the track and give up.

- Human love has died in a relationship and God's Love in our hearts is buried (sin).

- Both lovers stop loving—Matthew 24:12: "Agape shall wax cold."

Human love can become blessing

If Agape is the foundation of a marriage and is allowed to flow through each person, then all the human loves can be built and rebuilt and be the blessings God intended them to be all along—we only need one partner in order to do this.

If, however, Agape is quenched, then the relationship is only held together by human love, which is always unreliable.

Conclusion

It's critical to know the difference between human love and God's Love. When we are not loving with God's Love we must know how to turn around, "deal with" our sin, and become an open vessel.

Group Discussion Questions

1. Describe how God's Love differs from human love. (1 John 4:8; 1 Corinthians 13:4-8; Galatians 5:22-24; Romans 7:18)

    God's Love differs from human love in that everyone has human love. We are born with it. Hu- man love is a conditional, two-sided, bondage and self-centered love. Whereas God's Love is a supernatural gift we receive when we ask Him into our hearts. God's Love is a Love that keeps on coming no matter what happens.

    Human love only seeks the good of itself, and it's always dependent upon what we think, feel and want, what the other party does, and upon our circumstances. Whereas God's Love seeks only the good of the other person and it's only dependent upon God, who is always faithful, no matter how we feel or what we think. God's Love is the only solid foundation upon which we can build our lives and the only Love that can make us whole, give us our identity, meaning and purpose.

    (Pages 67, 72-73, 75, 77)

2. Briefly define the three human loves: *storge*, *phileo*, and *eros*. Give an example of each.

    Storge love is our natural, feeling love or our affection love. Storge love, however, can become a suffocating love or a controlling love. Eros love is our natural, sexual love (our "falling-in-love," love); it helps us to escape momentarily, but often distorts our self-reflection. Phileo love is our friendship love or whatever we have a strong attachment to.

    (Pages 68-73, 77-78)

3. Name four additional *characteristics* of human love described in this chapter.

    Human love is a *conditional* love because it always depends upon how we feel, what our circumstances are, and how the other person responds. It's a *two-sided* love because it always says "I'll love you if you love me, but if you stop loving me, I will stop loving you." It's a *bondage* love because it always causes us to have our own presumptions and expectations of the other person, then the other person is not free to respond from his heart, but out of his defenses. Lastly, it's a *self-centered* love because it always needs to get in return the love it so desperately desires.

    (Pages 67-68, 77)

4. Explain why human love is often referred to as a "need love."

    Human love is referred to as a "need love," because it always needs to be returned in order to be kept alive. It's always given in order to fulfill its own self-centered needs, wants and desires. All human loves, therefore, are "need" loves because they seek the good of themselves and not the other person.

    (Pages 68, 72)

5. What determines whether human love is good or bad? (1 Corinthians 3:11)

    The thing that determines whether human love is good or bad is the foundation upon which the human loves are based. If the human loves are built *upon God's Love* as a foundation, then they can become the blessings God intended them to be from the beginning. And then, when the humans loves fail, Agape will be there to carry us through and continue to reconcile us.

    If, however, the human loves are based on *self* (what we think, feel and want), then the natural loves will be conditional and reciprocal.

    Even if all the human loves have died in a relationship and only one person is willing to "agapao," there still is a possibility of restoring that relationship. However, if there is no willingness or openness to change and no Agape Love, then there's probably no hope for that relationship.

    (Pages 72-74)

6.   Summarize why it's so important to know the difference between God's Love and human love. (Matthew 24:12; Isaiah 59:2; 1 Corinthians 13:1-3; Song of Solomon 8:7)

It's important to know the difference between God's Love and human love because we need to recognize when we are functioning on God's Love and when we are not. And when we're not, we must realize we have quenched God's Spirit and it's sin. At this point we have a choice: we can continue on "led by the flesh" or we can confess that sin; turn around from following that sin and give that sin to God. Then all our other relationships won't suffer.

(Pages 67-68, 74-75, 78)

7.   Agape Love is "growing cold" in these end times. (Matthew 24:12) Why?

God's Love is growing cold in these end times because His Love has become buried under a ton of hurts, bitterness and resentments in our hearts and neither party is willing to be the first to change (let go). Both parties have chosen to "hold on to" their own justified hurts rather than to love God.

In these end times, God is allowing more trials in all our lives to toughen us up. Many of us however, prefer our "own" ways, over God's. Thus, God's Love is growing cold in our lives.

(Pages 74, 78)

8.   What should we do when we find we're not functioning on God's Love?

When we find that we are not functioning on God's Love, it's critical to immediately "deal with it," as 2 Corinthians 10:6 says. We deal with our sin by confessing it, repenting of it, and giving it to God.

(Page 74)

Personal Questions

1.   Have you or are you now experiencing any situations or struggles similar to those that were shared in this chapter? If so, describe them.

Open discussion.

Ask questions like:

•   Are you functioning on storge love (possessing and clutching people)?

•   Do you have a fear of losing control of people?

•   Are you staying in your marriage for protection only?

(Pages 68-72)

2.   Describe the kind of love you most often function on. Be honest.

Open discussion.

Ask questions like:

- Do you fear losing your family's love?

- Are you always looking for another's love?

- Do you have strong attachments to things?

3.   Phileo love is the *result* of an **intimate relationship**. However, with Agape, the **Love** comes *first* and then the **relationship** follows. (John 15:13-15)

4.   Has your love for God and others been dependent upon how you feel, what your circumstances are, and how the other person responds? Explain.

Open discussion.

5.   Using 1 Corinthians 12:31 and 1 Corinthians 13:1-4, 13, explain why loving God's Way is so important.

If we don't learn to love as God desires (the more "excellent way"), we will have wasted our lives and, as 1 Corinthians 13 says, "We will be nothing." God's Love is the only Love that can make us whole and give our lives meaning and purpose.

(Pages 57, 75)

6.   Is there an area in your life right now where you can apply this teaching? If so, where?

Open discussion.

Continue at Home

1.   Write on a note card all the Scriptures that particularly ministered to you in this chapter. Use them to apply these principles. Memorize them.

2.   Ask God to show you the times you begin to trust in your own ability to love (human love) rather than depending upon Him for His Love. Recognize these times and deal with your thoughts and emotions in the proper way. Be prepared to share examples.

3.   This week, note in your journal the different types of human love you experience.

READ:	MEMORIZE:
1 Corinthians 13	Romans 7:18
Romans 5	Isaiah 59:2
Matthew 24	1 John 4:8

Chapter 6: True Identity and Security
DVD 1 Session 2 -20 minutes

Our two basic needs

- Our two basic needs are the need to be loved and the need to love.

- Both needs can be fulfilled only by God and His Love.

- He must be the total provision for all our needs—no matter where we are walking (married, divorced, single, separated).

- Our two basic needs can *never* be fulfilled by others, things or accomplishments.

Our need to *be loved*

- It's fulfilled by our knowing that God loves us unconditionally.

- This is what gives us our true identity and security.

- God's Love is the foundation upon which we build our lives.

- We are loved not because of what we do, but because of who we are in Him.

- God's Love will never fail—His Love just keeps on coming no matter what we do.

- If there is sin, His Love will be blocked from flowing into our lives, but nothing will ever separate us from His Love in our hearts.

Our need *to love*

- It's fulfilled by our loving God and others.

- This is what gives our lives meaning and purpose. (We will cover this further in Chapter 8 and 15-16.)

Insecure in God's Love

- If our identity is not in God's Love, then, when we fail we will sink because we think no one (including God) will ever love us again.

- Trying to earn everyone's love becomes our motivation.

Secure in God's Love

- If our identity is in God's Love, then when we fail it's okay because who we are is still intact and we can pick up the pieces and go on.

- God will use our failures as a way of binding us closer.

- We will understand His Love for us to a deeper degree.

Group Discussion Questions

1. Man has two basic needs. Define them and explain how they can be fulfilled. (1 Corinthians 13:2c; Jeremiah 31:3; 1 John 3:14; 4:12)

    Man's two basic needs are the need *to be loved*, which is fulfilled by our knowing that God loves us (giving us our identity and security); and the need *to love*, which is fulfilled by our loving God and others (giving us our meaning and purpose).

    (Pages 81, 89)

2. Consider if these two needs can ever be permanently met by others, things, or accomplishments. (Philippians 4:19; 1 Corinthians 3:11; Psalm 73:25) Share your thoughts.

    Our need *to be loved* can never be permanently fulfilled by people, things, or accomplishments. Only God can continuously supply all our needs.

    (Pages 81, 89)

3. If God's Love *has become* our total identity and security, what happens to us when we stumble and fall? What happens to us if His Love *is not* our complete security?

    If God's Love has become our complete security and identity and we know that He loves us no matter what, then we won't be shaken to the core if the people we love let us down or are taken away from us. Psalms 73:25 says there should be "none upon the earth that (we) desire besides Thee."

    However, if God's Love is not our complete security and identity, then when the people we love let us down or are taken from us, everything collapses because who we are was built upon these people and these things, and not God's Love as it should be. Our confidence needs to be in God and how much He loves us and not in ourselves, in others, or in our accomplishments.

    (Pages 82-85)

4. When we sin and do something that causes God's Spirit to be quenched in us, what happens to God's Love in our hearts? (Matthew 24:12; Ephesians 4:30a; 1 John 1:9)

    God's Love in our hearts never stops coming, 1 Corinthians 13:8 tells us ("it never fails"). In other words, nothing can ever separate us from the Love of the Father in our hearts (Romans 8:38-39). However, when we sin, His Love in our hearts will be quenched, covered and prevented from flowing out into our lives (our souls).

    (2nd printing, pages 85, 89)

Personal Questions

1. Our need *to be loved* brings us our **security** and our **identity**. (Isaiah 49;16; 54:10; Hebrews 13:5) Our need *to love* brings us our **meaning** and our **purpose**. (1 Timothy 1:5; Philippians 1:21; 1 John 4:12) Give personal examples of each.

    (1 Timothy 1:5; Philippians 1:21; 1 John 4:12) Give personal examples of each.

    My "personal" example is in Chapter 6, "Shattered." When my ministry collapsed, my identity and security did also. God wanted to show me that nothing can come before Him in importance—not even a ministry. God had to remove the hindrances in my own life that prevented His Love, and show me that He loves me regardless of what I ever do for Him. He loves me unconditionally. Only then did I have the security (of His Love) to begin to love others the way I am supposed to.

    (Pages 82-85)

2. On what do you depend for your identity and security? Give examples. What happens when these things change or let you down?

    Open discussion.

    Ask questions like:

    Do you base your identity on your husband, your family members, your children, your name, your intelligence, your looks, your personality, or any other personal abilities?

3. Summarize what you tend to rely upon to fulfill your need for meaning and purpose. Do these things ever disappoint you?

    Ask questions like: Do you tend to rely upon your career, your ministry, your schooling, etc.?

4. READ John 14:15-21, 23 and John 15:1-10. Briefly describe why we also need *to love*. (Galatians 5:14)

    If we love (agapao) God, He then will manifest Himself to us and through us and we'll be able to love others as He desires. God's purpose for all of us is to love (i.e., to bring forth fruit). There is no way, however, that we will be able to love others unless we first love God. Once we love God, we'll receive His Love not only for ourselves, but also to pass on to others. This is what then will give our lives meaning and purpose.
    (Pages 82-84)

5. Is there an area in your life right now where you can apply this teaching? If so, what area?

    Open discussion (spouse, children, family, relatives, friends, bosses).

Continue at Home

1.   On a note card, write out the Scriptures that particularly ministered to you in this chapter. Use them to help you apply these principles. Memorize them.

2.   Every day this week, make a special time to be with the Lord. Choose to give Him all your expectations, desires, and emotional needs. Ask Him to meet these needs and give you His Life. Once you are a cleansed vessel, ask Him to help you put the interests of others (your spouse, family, etc.) above your own.

3.   Write out on 3x5 note cards the "Who I Am in Christ" Scriptures from the Supplemental Study Notes section of this book. Pick the ones that particularly minister to you and memorize them.

READ: MEMORIZE:
Isaiah 43   John 15:16
Philippians 1   Ephesians 1:4
Psalm 18   Galatians 2:20
Colossians 1:21   Philippians 1:21

Chapter 7: Knowing God Loves Us
DVD 1 - Session 2 - 18 minutes

The importance of knowing God's Love

- If we know God loves us, we can do anything; without His Love we are nothing.

- We can't go further in God's Way of Love (can't love Him or others) until we know He loves us.

- Then we will have the confidence and the trust to lay down our wills and lives to Him.

- His Love is the foundation of our faith. We must experience His Love for us before we can lay down our lives and love others.

- God's Love is a gift we all receive when we accept Jesus into our hearts.

- His Love is the only thing that will give us hope for the future—it's what helps us persevere through the trials.

If we know God loves us

- We can continually lay down our wills and lives to Him and love Him in return.

- Then we will daily experience His Life through us.

- We will not fear what He might allow in our lives.

If we doubt God's Love

- We won't have the confidence or the trust to lay our lives down to God and love Him.

- Then we won't experience His Love, either for ourselves or for others.

- And we won't have that daily experience of His Life through us.

How can we prove God loves us?

- God says so in His Word—His Word is truth and we must believe it.

- God sent His Son to die for our sins, so we could be reconciled to Him.

- God sent His Spirit into our lives to bear witness of His great Love for us.

- God has given us Abundant Life, which is His supernatural Love, Wisdom and Power, and He wants us to experience this Life in place of our own.

How does God communicate His Love to us?

- By our daily reading His Word—this is how He speaks to us.

- Through our Christian brothers and sisters—we are extensions of His Love to each other.

- By our circumstances—all are "Father-filtered."

Basic problem: most Christians don't *know* (*oida*) God

- Knowing God means having living experience of Him in our lives—seeing His handprint in all our circumstances.

- Knowing God is experiencing His Love and His Life through us.

Group Discussion Questions

1. Share *why knowing God loves us* is the first step in living God's Way of Agape. (1 Corinthians 3:11; 1 John 4:19; Hebrews 13:5; 2 Timothy 1:12b)

    Knowing God loves us is the foundation of our whole Christian walk. If we know that God loves us (experientially), then we will have the confidence and the trust to lay our wills and our lives down to Him and love Him in return. However, if we don't know that He loves us, we won't be able to move forward in our faith walk. We can't lay our wills and our lives down to someone if we don't think they really love us.

    (Pages 91, 95, 105)

2. Describe several ways that we can *know* God loves us. (Jeremiah 31:3; 1 John 4:10; John 3:16; Romans 5:5; 8:16; John 10:10)

    We know that God loves us because:

    - God says so in His Word.

    - He sent Jesus to die for us and to give us His own personal Love.

    - We receive His Spirit in our hearts as a down payment of His Love.

    - He has given us His Abundant Life.

    (Pages 96-98, 101, 105)

3. How does God communicate His Love to us? (Psalm 119:159-160; 1 John 3:16; Isaiah 43:1-4) Give examples.

    God communicates His Love to us by:

    - Our daily reading His Word.

    - Our Christian brothers and sisters loving us.

- His loving us through our situations and circumstances.

(Pages 99-101, 105)

4. Knowing God loves us gives us *hope* for the future. Why? (Jeremiah 29:11; 1 John 3:2; Hebrews 6:19)

If we know someone loves us, we can always go forward. We will have the confidence and the trust to pick up the pieces and start again. Hope is the ability to trust God in every situation and to look beyond our current circumstance. This hope is our anchor for the future.

(Pages 82-87, 99, 105-106)

Share the example of Diana Bantlow in Chapter 7, "All Your Hairs Are Numbered."

Personal Questions

1. Are you experiencing a daily, personal, and intimate relationship with God? Do you *know* His Love? (Ephesians 3:17-19; Psalm 86:5-7; 27:5, 13) If not, ask God what is blocking you from knowing Him and experiencing His Love. (Be sure to note the things He shows you this week.)

Ask questions like:

- Do you see God's hand in everything?

- Are you experiencing His Love in your personal life?

Pray and ask God to search your heart and reveal what He wants you to give to Him, so you can experience His Love to a greater degree.

2. Are you aware of any negative thoughts and emotions that are preventing you from experiencing God's Love?

Open discussion.

Examples: fear, guilt, anxiety, worry, anger, criticalness, self-pity

(Page 178)

3. Summarize why is it so critical to give these negative thoughts over to God. (Isaiah 59:2; Matthew 16:24-25; 2 Corinthians 4:10-11; Philippians 1:20-21) How does knowing that God loves you help you to lay these things aside? (Psalm 37:23-24)

It's critical to give these negative things over to God, because we must remain an open and cleansed vessel so He can love others through us. If we love Him, we can then continue on in God's Way of Love. However, if we don't relinquish these self-centered things, we'll quench His Life and His Love in our hearts.

(Pages 82-84, 92, 94-95)

4.   What key points in this chapter are you still struggling with or having difficulty with?

Open discussion.

Ask questions like:

*   Are you struggling with knowing that God loves you?

*   Does God communicate His Love to you? How?

*   Do you have living experience of God's Love daily?

*   Can you say "Though He slay me, yet will I trust Him?"

(Page 101)

5.   If we really knew how much God loves us, we would never **fear** what God would allow in our lives. (Isaiah 43:1-4; Matthew 10:29-31; 2 Timothy 1:7) Are there any situations in your life right now that are causing you to fear? How does *knowing that God loves you personally* change your attitude about these situations?

God's Word says that He loves us and that He has not given us a spirit of fear, but of Love and a sound mind. Therefore, if we know He loves us and we have the confidence to give our fears to Him, then we will always have hope for the future, regardless of what our circumstances or our situations are telling us.

(Page 85)

6.   Is there an area in your life right now where you can apply this teaching? If so, what area?

Can you apply this teaching:

*   In your daily walk with Him?

*   In your reading of His Word?

*   In recognizing His loving hand in all your circumstances?

Continue at Home

1.   Over the next week, ask God to enable you to experience His love in a new way. Be sure your heart and life are cleansed.

2.   Write out the Scriptures from the Knowing God Loves Me chart in the Supplemental Notes at the back of the textbook. Write them on 3x5 cards and put your own name before each of the verses. As you read the Scriptures aloud, choose to believe what God is saying to you personally.

READ: MEMORIZE:
1 John 3   1 John 4:10
John 14 and 15   Isaiah 43:1b-2, 5
Psalm 18   Hebrews 13:6
Isaiah 43   John 17:26

Chapter 8: What Does It Mean to Love God?
DVD 2 Session 3 - 53 minutes

Basic need to love

- It's fulfilled only by our learning to love God and others.

- This is what gives our lives meaning and purpose.

To love (agapao) means

- To totally give ourselves over to something.

- To be totally consumed with something.

- It's what we put first in our lives.

- It's a commitment love—it's submitting our wills and our lives to something.

- We can love (agapao) God, man, or things of the world.

- This is completely different from *Agape*, which is God's pure, unconditional Love.

To love (agapao) God means

- To lose self—all our own thoughts, emotions and desires that are contrary to God's—thus, becoming an open and cleansed vessel.

- To put His Will and His Desires above our own.

- Allowing His Life to become our own.

- This is not an emotional love (storge), but a commitment love.

Three steps of loving God

- Choosing to obey His Word, not our own thoughts and feelings.

  - Relinquishing what we think, feel and want, and doing what He desires.

  - *Denying ourselves*—barring ourselves from following the flesh.

  - Obedience is the only answer.

- Trusting God to perform His Will through us, not our own ability and power.

  - Relying upon Him (with unreserved confidence) to accomplish His Will in our lives, no matter how we feel or what we think.

  - *Picking up our crosses*—and doing what He has asked, regardless of our circumstances.

- He will align our feelings to match what we have chosen.

- He makes us genuine.

- Truth is where the word and the deed match and become one.

- Worshipping and serving God.

  - Worshipping means prostrating ourselves before God (inside)—serving God means presenting our bodies as living sacrifices (outside).

  - *Following God*—cleaving unto Him, binding ourselves with Him so that we become one. Obedient unto death.

He is our Life

- When we become one with God (one heart, will and soul), then it's God's Life that comes forth and not our own.

- It's God's character, not our own.

- Jesus is not just *in* our lives at this moment, *He is our Life*!

Group Discussion Questions

1. Define the Greek word *agapao* (to love). (John 12:24; Ephesians 5:2b; Luke 9:23) How does *agapao* differ from *storge* or *phileo* love?

   The Greek word *agapao* means "totally given over to"; "completely consumed with"; or, "putting first in our lives." To *agapao* something is to bind ourselves with something and become one with it.

   Agapao is our commitment love; whereas storge is our feeling (or affection) love; and, phileo is our friendship (or having something in common) love.

   (Pages 68-73, 110-113, 129)

2. Describe the difference between the verb *agapao* that we are studying here and the noun *Agape* that we studied in Chapter 3. (1 John 4:8b)

   The verb *agapao* means to totally give ourselves over to something. We can *agapao* God, man, or things of the world. Whereas, the noun *Agape* is always (throughout Scripture) God's pure, unconditional Love. There is never a negative usage of this supernatural Love.

   (Page 110)

3. Can we *agapao* bad things? Give some contemporary examples. (Matthew 22:37-39; John 3:19; 12:43; Luke 6:32)

   Yes, we can agapao things that don't glorify God. We can love (agapao) our careers, our houses, our money, pleasure, and ourselves.

   (Pages 110-111)

4. Summarize the three steps of loving God. (Matthew 4:1-10; Philippians 2:8; Luke 22:42; Luke 14:26-27; 2 Corinthians 4:11; Luke 5:11; Romans 12:1)

    To love God means to:

    Obey God's Word by setting aside our own thoughts and emotions, saying, "Not my will, but Thine." Trust God's Power to perform His Word by relying upon His ability to perform His Will, not my own. Worship and serve God only, by following and binding ourselves to Him.

    (Pages 112-124)

5. Explain what it means to become one with God. (1 John 4:17; Philippians 1:21; Galatians 2:20) How does this happen?

    Becoming one with God means choosing to follow, cleave and so bind ourselves with Him, that we become one heart, one will and one life. Becoming one with God is loving Him the way He desires—totally giving ourselves over to Him with all our heart, will and soul.

    (Pages 109-110, 113)

Personal Questions

1. Describe some of the things in your own life that you *agapao*. Be specific.

    Open discussion. Ask them if they "agapao" their children, house, career, themselves, pleasure, etc..

2. READ: Matthew 16:24. Write out this verse and memorize it. What are the three steps of loving God mentioned here?

    The verse is: "If any man will come after Me, let him *deny himself* and *pick up his cross and follow Me.*"

    Deny self— this means to obey God's Word, not our own emotions and thoughts. Take up our cross—this means to trust God's power to perform His Will in our lives. Follow Him—this means to become one with God (one heart, will and soul).

    (Page 113)

3. What must we do before God's Love can be manifested through us to others? (John 12:24; 15:3-4; Luke 14:26; Ephesians 5:2; 1 John 3:16)

    In order to love others, we must first love (agapao) God. We need to choose to set aside our "self" (the flesh) and become open and cleansed vessels. This is the denying of ourselves and becoming one heart, will and soul with God. Once we have done this, then we can go on and love others.

    (Pages 113-116, 123-126)

4. In your own life, what are some of the negative thoughts, emotions, and desires that are the most difficult for you to deny or bar yourself from following? What

happens when you give in to these thoughts and feelings and choose to follow them?

Open discussion.

In my own life, the hardest negative thoughts and emotions to deny are the ones I am "justified" (by the world's standards) in feeling. Much of the time, they are things that have happened over and over again.

Also, I find it difficult to "bar myself from following" certain inherent fears and insecurities that I have. Even if I open myself up for a moment and entertain these things, I paralyze my walk with Him.

5.   Are there areas in your life right now where you are having difficulty trusting God because of your feelings, your situation or another person's responses? Explain.

Open discussion.

Continue at Home

1.   Write on a note card the Scriptures that particularly ministered to you in this chapter. Use them to help you apply these principles. Memorize them.

2.   Over the next week, ask God to show you the areas where you are not loving Him. Write down in your journal what He shows you. Ask Him to help you the next time these areas come up to choose to obey Him, trust Him, and follow Him, rather than give in to your "old ways."

3.   The reality of denying ourselves is a painful and difficult task. It is impossible to accomplish apart from Christ working in us. Our responsibility is only to be willing— willing to continually yield ourselves to Christ and allow Him to do the job through us. Ask God to continually reveal your own willingness (or unwillingness) to "die to self." Note what He shows you in your journal.

READ:	MEMORIZE:
Hosea 1-3	John 12:24-26
John 14	John 14:21, 23
1 John 4	Philippians 2:7-8
Philippians 2:5-11	Luke 22:42
Galatians 2:20	
Matthew 10:39	

Chapter 9: Satan's Three Temptations
DVD 2 Session 3 -12 minutes

Satan tries to keep us from loving (agapao) God by

- Tempting us *not* to obey God's Will, but our own desires.

  - Our response should be "There is no other way to live."

  - We must obey God's voice and not our own thoughts and feelings.

- Tempting us *not* to trust God's Power to perform in our lives, but our own abilities.

  - Our response should be "We will trust the Holy Spirit."

  - He will perform God's Will in His way and in His timing.

- Tempting us *not* to worship and serve God only, but to follow our flesh and things of the world.

  - Our response should be "We will not follow or bind ourselves to anyone or anything else but God."

(A temptation is something that causes us to choose either God's Way or our own.)

Satan wants our faith

- Our faith is built on the faithfulness (trustworthiness) of God.

- If Satan can cause doubt and unbelief in these areas, he has won.

- It takes faith to love God.

- Our faith is the only victory that will allow all things in our lives to be "born of God."

Group Discussion Questions

1. Why is Satan so intent upon keeping us from experiencing "abundant life?" (Ephesians 3:19; Romans 8:2-6)

   Satan is intent upon keeping us from experiencing "abundant Life" because he doesn't want God's Life to be passed on. Experiencing God's Life not only increases our faith but also brings others to Christ. Satan will do everything in his power to prevent this. (Pages 140, 143) (Pages 136-137)

2. Satan does not want us to love God. Summarize the three temptations he constantly throws at us.

   Satan's three temptations are:

   1) Don't obey God's Word, but give in to and follow your own feelings and desires.

2) Don't trust God to perform His Will in your life, but depend upon your own ability— do it your own way.

3) Don't follow God, but totally give yourself over to your own thoughts, emotions and desires—put yourself first.

(Pages 133-134, 137)

3. Why does God allow these temptations in our lives? (Deuteronomy 8:2; 30:19; 13:3-4)

God allows these temptations in our lives because He wants to see if we love Him and also to strengthen our faith. Our faith is the only victory that overcomes and allows "all" things to be born of God. We need to learn to be strong and to continue to relinquish our lives to God, so that we can retain the victory.

God uses Satan and his wiles as a tool to expose and unearth the sin in our own lives. If we can see it, then we can "deal with it" and be freed from it forever.

(Pages 137 and also 225)

4. How does Jesus' refusal of Satan's temptations illustrate John 12:23-26 and 2 Corinthians 4:11-12?

By refusing Satan's temptations, Jesus remained an open and cleansed vessel. Thus, He was able to bring forth much fruit—the Father's Love to us.

(Pages 133-134)

5. Jesus resisted Satan and was obedient through the power of God's Word. According to James 1:21-25, how is God's Word to work in our lives?

As we choose to set aside the flesh and become cleansed vessels, we will be able to hear and receive God's Word. As we then not only "hear God's Word" but become "doers of that Word," James says we will be blessed (happy) in all we do.

Personal Questions

1. READ: Matthew 4:1-10. Write out Satan's three temptations and translate them into your own words.

    • **Matthew 4:1-4**: "Command that these stones be made bread." (In other words, do what you want, feel and desire.)

    • **Matthew 4:5-8**: "Cast Yourself down: for it is written, He shall give his angels charge concerning thee." (In other words, don't trust God to work in your life, rely on your own power and strength.)

    • **Matthew 4:8-10**: "All these things will I give Thee, if You will fall down and worship me." (In other words, "totally give yourself over to" and "follow" Satan.)

(Pages 133-134)

2.   As you look at your own life, can you see any examples of Satan's three temptations?

Open discussion.

Look for thoughts like: "Do what you want, don't take time to be a cleansed vessel. Tell them how you feel. Do it NOW!" "Do this thing on your own. You don't need anyone else. Say and do what you feel is appropriate." "You're all that counts. You are number one. Think about how you feel; it doesn't matter about him!"

3.   From Matthew 4:1-10, write out Jesus' rebuttals to Satan's temptations. Memorize them. (See Deuteronomy 8:17; 6:16; Exodus 17:7 for explanation of second temptation.)

   1)   "Man shall not live by bread (physical things) alone, but by every word that proceeds out of the mouth of God." In other words, the only way we can live is by *obeying God's Word*, not our own feelings and desires.

   2)   "Thou shalt not tempt the Lord thy God." In other words, don't test God by trying to do what He asked in our own strength. (Note: Deut 8:17; 6:16 and Exodus 17:7 for background explanation.)

   3)   "You shall worship the Lord thy God, and Him only shall you serve." In other words, we're not to follow or bind ourselves to anything else but God.

(Pages 133-134)

Continue at Home

1.   Write down the Scriptures that particularly ministered to you in this chapter. Use them to help you apply these principles. Memorize them.

2.   Write out James 1:12-15. Summarize what James is saying.

3.   Watch this week for Satan's temptations. Note them and choose, instead, to love God.

READ:
James 1
Deuteronomy 8
Deuteronomy 30:15-20

Chapter 10: "Ye Are the Temple of God"
Session 4 - DVD 2 - 1hr, 7 minutes

What does it mean to love God with all our heart, mind and soul?

- "Mind" here is "dianoia"—dianoia means willpower.

- God is a God of great detail—something specific is meant by each of these terms.

- We need to understand these concepts so we can love Him the way He desires.

We are the temple of God

- In the Old Testament, the Shekinah Glory dwelt in the physical Temple of Solomon—now God's Spirit dwells in us.

- There is a correlation between Solomon's Temple and believers.

- Solomon's Temple is a model, blueprint, or "type" of a believer indwelt by the Holy Spirit.

- Solomon's Temple was special.

- It was the only Temple where detailed plans of construction and furniture were given by God.

- It was the only Temple where God's Spirit dwelt permanently.

- It was the only Temple where Ark of the Covenant dwelt.

- By studying the floor plan of this Temple, we will understand exactly what our spirit, heart, will, and soul are and thus be able to love God as He desires.

The Temple as a blueprint of a believer (see Charts)

- **Holy of Holies**—*New* spirit of a believer (pneuma).

  - Spirit is the new life source of a believer.

  - New energy source—new power source.

- **Holy Place**—*New* heart of a believer (kardia).

  - Place where God's Life is begun.

  - Totally new heart—with God's supernatural Love, Wisdom and Power.

  - Our old heart, before being born again is evil and corrupt.

    - It will always be self-centered and proud—it's the old man.

    - No one can understand it or cure it—no hope for the future.

- Our new heart, after being born again, is "Christ in us, our hope of glory"—the hidden man of the heart.

- Our heart is the center core or foundation of our whole person.

- **Porch**—*New* willpower of believer (dianoia).

  - This is our will and the power to perform it.

  - It's the key to our Christian walk because it determines whose life will be lived in our souls.

  - It's the passageway or the doorway for God's Life in our hearts to flow out into our lives. This door can be opened or it can be closed. *Dia* means "channel"—*noia* means "of the mind" (spirit).

  - Our willpower has two parts:

    - God's supernatural Will and Power, is where He counsels us as to what His Will is, and then gives us the power to perform it.

    - The second part of our willpower is our free choice, where we have the freedom to follow what God has shown us, or we can choose our own will and trust in our own ability to perform.

- Temple porch also had two parts:

  - Golden vestibule which represents God's supernatural Will and Power.

  - Bronze pillars which represent our own free choice.

    - These pillars had names, Jackin and Boaz. The pillars represent choices made "in His counsel" (Jackin) and "by His might" (Boaz).

- We constantly have two choices facing us:

  - Faith choices—choosing by faith to follow what God wants, saying, "Not my will, but Thine."

  - Emotional choices—choosing to follow what we want, feel and desire over what God wants.

- **Inner Court**—soul (not yet redeemed) (psyche).

  - Two parts to our soul:

    - Our conscious thoughts, emotions and desires.

    - Our subconscious (hidden chambers).

  - Our soul is the outward expression of our lives—our visible life.

  - Our soul life differs from our heart life:

    - Life is brought into existence in our hearts.

- Life is then expressed or shown forth in our souls.

- Heart life is invisible—soul life is visible.

- Heart life is like the roots of a plant—soul life is like the beautiful flowers we can see.

  - Our soul is a neutral area that can either be filled with God's Life from our hearts (if we have made faith choices), or with self-life (if we have made emotional choices).

  - God desires our souls to show forth His Life—His Love becoming our love, His Thoughts, our thoughts and His Power, our own.

    - This is being Spirit-filled.

    - This is single-mindedness—one life is being lived.

  - However, when we make emotional choices, God's Life in our hearts becomes quenched and the soul life that is produced is our own self-life.

    - This is Double-mindedness—double souled.

    - Two lives are being lived here.

  - Where does "self-life" come from?

    - It comes from the hurts, resentments and things that we have never dealt with (never given to God), but just pushed down in hidden chambers.

  - Soul and body are unredeemed—whereas our spirit, heart and willpower are already re- stored.

    - Note Temple: Holy of Holies, Holy Place and Porch are gold—which represents God's holy and pure nature.

    - Pillars, Inner and Outer courts, however, are bronze—which represents something that still needs to be judged (sin is present). Hidden chambers are wooden—which represents something that needs to be burned up.

  - Soul and body are in a sanctification process.

    - A process by which we learn to set aside all that is of the flesh.

    - Put off the old man—and put on Christ.

  - Putting on Christ in our lives is a moment-by-moment process.

    - The "new man" is Christ's Life in our hearts, which we must daily put on in our lives.

- **Outer Court**—our bodies (soma).

- Our bodies are the vehicle or carrier for the expression of our lives.

- Our souls and bodies cannot be separated.

- As we "walk by the Spirit"—our bodies will show forth God's Life.

- As we "walk after the flesh"—our bodies will show forth self-life.

    • Power of sin is an energy force that dwells in our unredeemed bodies and continually causes us to "miss the mark."

- The war that goes on between power of sin and Power of God is waged in our souls.

- Christ in our heart is the only overcoming power to free us from this war.

God wants us Spirit-filled

• Just like Solomon's Temple was filled from the inside out, this is what God desires for us.

• He wants the Holy Spirit to come forth from our hearts and fill our souls. (see John 7:38)

• In order to do this, we must learn how to love (agapao) Him with all our heart, will and soul—how to become one heart, will and soul with Him.

Definition of Terms (see Glossary)

• Flesh—The part of our old human nature (soul and body) that has not been redeemed yet. It is the residue (remainder, leftover garbage, dross) that still remains in our soul from the "old man."

• Old Man—This is the old human heart, the part of our old human nature that was destroyed at our new birth and replaced with a totally new heart.*

• New Heart—The brand-new heart (new nature) that God gives us when we are born again is Christ in us, "our hope of glory." This new heart is filled with God's supernatural Life: His Love, Wisdom and Power.

• New Man—We are to "put on" Christ's Life (from our hearts) in our souls daily, making us a new man.

[*The "putting off" of the old man can be said to be twofold: positionally (in our hearts) at our conversion and experientially (in our souls) in the gradual process of sanctification.]

Group Discussion Questions

1. What is the purpose of comparing Solomon's Temple with our bodies? Does

seeing the Temple of God graphically enable you to love God more? (1
Corinthians 6:19-20; 3:16; 1 Kings 8:10-11) Why do we use Solomon's Temple as
a model of the New Testament believer? Why not use Herod's or Nehemiah's
Temple? (1 Chronicles 28:11-12, 19-20)

The purpose of using Solomon's Temple and comparing it to our bodies is so that
we might understand a little more clearly what our heart, will and soul are. Then we
can go on and love God in each of these areas as He desires.

Having a clearer understanding of what happens when we sin and quench God's
Spirit encourages us to confess, turn around, and become that cleansed vessel
more quickly—thus, loving Him as He desires.

The reason we use Solomon's Temple as a model of a New Testament believer is
because it was unique and special. It was the only temple where: 1) The plans of
the construction and the furniture were given to David by the Spirit of God; 2)
God's Spirit dwelt permanently; and, 3) The Ark of the Covenant stood.

(Page 143)

2.   Describe the *new heart* we receive as a result of being born again. (Ezekiel 36:25-
27; 1 Peter 3:4; Romans 5:5; Colossians 1:27; 1 John 5:11-12) What was our heart
life like *before* we were born again? (Jeremiah 17:9; Isaiah 47:10d; Genesis 8:21d;
Mark 7:21)

The new Heart that God gives us when we're born again is the place where God's
Life is created and begun. When we're born again, we receive a totally new
heart—a heart that now consists of God's supernatural Love, His supernatural
Wisdom, and His supernatural Strength. This is God's own Eternal Life.

Our "heart life" before we were born again was evil and corrupt from birth. It's self-
centered, proud and will never seek God on it's own (Isaiah 47:10). Jeremiah 17:9
says our old heart is deceitful above all things and incurably wicked—no one will
ever understand it.

(Pages 148-153, 170-171)

3.   With this in mind, can we have real and lasting life change before we are born
again? Why/Why not? (Jeremiah 17:9) Do you have any personal examples?

Scripture tells us that we cannot have any real and lasting change before we are
born again. The reason is that we do not have another "power source" within us to
produce permanent change—or produce anything different than what we naturally
think and feel.

Without God's Spirit and a new heart, we can never "inwardly" change, no matter
how much we want to. Once we are born again, however, we receive a new power
source (God's Spirit) to en- able us to produce real and lasting inward change.

(Page 151 example)

4.   Our new "heart life" is God's supernatural Life. Describe what this is. (Romans 5:5;

Hebrews 8:10; Galatians 4:6) If the only life that now exists in our hearts is God's Life, what part of us still needs constant transformation? (Romans 12:1-2; 1 Corinthians 6:20; 2 Corinthians 4:16)

God's supernatural Life is God's supernatural Love, Wisdom and Power.

Our soul is the inward part of us that still needs constant transformation. This can only happen as we learn to really love (agapao) God. See Charts 5 and 6.

(Pages 159, 161)

5.   Describe our soul. What is its function? (1 Corinthians 6:20; Ephesians 5:17-18; 2 Corinthians 4:10) What's the difference between "heart life" and "soul life"? (Proverbs 4:23; Isaiah 58:10-11)

Our soul is made up of our thoughts, emotions and desires (conscious and unconscious). Our soul is mainly the outward expression of our lives—it's what we see and feel coming from each other.

The function of our soul, I believe, is to reflect Christ's Life: His Love, His Wisdom and His Power.

The difference between heart life and soul life is: heart life is created, started and begun in our hearts and it's invisible (no one can see it but God), whereas our soul life is "manifested" (shown forth) life that others can see and hear. Soul life is visible life.

(Pages 156-158)

6.   If, as born-again believers, we have God's Life in our hearts, where does our "self life" come from? (Proverbs 5:22; John 8:34; Romans 6:16)

Self life comes from the hurts, resentments, bitterness, etc., that we have never dealt with before, but have simply buried in our secret hidden chambers (our subconscious). Self-life is triggered when we choose to follow what these things are telling us to do rather than what God wants.

(Pages 160-162)

7.   Colossians 3:8-10 tells us we are to "put off" the old man and "put on" the new. What exactly does this mean? (Ephesians 4:22-24; Romans 6:11-13) Scripturally, what is this process called?

Putting off the "old man" means putting off (destroying, getting rid of) the old, unconverted self, the old me. We do this positionally (in our hearts) at our conversion and experientially (in our souls) in our daily choices to set aside what we think, feel and desire so that God's Life can come forth. This is the "putting on" of the new man—the new me.

The process of putting off the old man and putting on the new is called "sanctification."

(Pages 162-163)

8.   Describe what "walking after the flesh" means. (Galatians 5:17-21) What does "walking after the spirit" mean? (Galatians 5:22-25) Give examples.

Personal Questions

1.   For each part of Solomon's Temple listed below, name the corresponding part in the born-again believer:

     Holy of Holies = **New Spirit**   Inner Court = **Soul**

     Holy Place = **New Heart**   Outer Court = **Body**

     Porch = **New Willpower**   Hidden Chambers = **Subconscious**

     (Page 146)

2.   Which Temple chart most appropriately describes you the majority of the time? When do you tend to be *single-minded*? *Double-minded*? Give examples.

     Open discussion.

     Ask questions like: Do you stumble on the big things of life, or is it those little daily hassles that seem to push you over?

3.   Have you ever personally experienced God's Love flowing through you to another person when you knew you had none of your own to give? How about God's Wisdom? His Power?

Continue at Home

1.   Conduct an experiment: Watch for incidents in your life this week where you experience being Chart 5—single-minded, showing forth God, and walking after His Spirit. Also note this week the times you are Chart 6. When you recognize this, stop, pray, identify the problem, confess it, repent of it, give it to God, and get into His Word. Be prepared to share the results of your experiment.

     READ or MEMORIZE:
     Ezekiel 36:26
     Philippians 2:13
     Romans 6:6-7
     Ephesians 5:17-18
     1 Corinthians 6:20

Chapter 11: Loving God With All Our Heart
DVD 3 - Session 5 - 25 minutes

Nature of our hearts

- Our heart is the center core of our whole being.

- It's the place where our thoughts, emotions and desires are started and begun.

- Our heart is the foundation block upon which everything else is built.

- All continuing activity depends upon the life that resides in our heart.

Loving God with all our heart means two things

- Making our initial choice to give God our heart and becoming one heart with Him—receiving His Life into our hearts (His Love, His Wisdom and His Power).

- Continually allowing His Life from our heart to be the motivation for all we choose to do—doing the Will of God from our hearts.

Fountain of living water

- God's Life in our hearts "should be" like a fountain of water springing forth and filling our lives.

- When we make emotional choices, however:

  - God's Life is quenched and unable to come forth.

  - Our hearts are covered with "grease."

  - And God's pure fountain of water is blocked.

What is sin?

- Anything that causes us to be separated from God.

- Any choice that is not of faith.

  - These things then cover our heart with grease and form a barrier that prevents God from coming forth.

- The original negative thought is not sin, it's what we choose to do with that thought that makes it sin or not.

Pride

- Pride is following what we think and feel over what God is telling us to do.

- Pride is not loving (agapao) God, but ourselves.

- It's totally giving ourselves over to what we think, feel and desire.

Four types of hearts

- Unbeliever

    - Unregenerate heart—Word of God is fallen "by the wayside" (not in heart).

    - Hardened heart—Receives Word of God, but has no root and falls away.

- Believer

    - Sin-covered heart—None of God's Love flowing because cares of this life have choked it out.

    - Pure heart—Because this person loves God, he brings forth much fruit (doing the Will of God from his heart).

Knowing God's Will

- We must read His Word to know His Will.

- God's Words are God's thoughts—it's how He talks to us and counsels us.

- We must not limit God to our interpretation of His Word.

    - His promises don't always come about as we understand.

    - God often has larger spiritual purposes.

- If you must move quickly:

    - Pray and acknowledge God is in control.

    - Tell God you're not sure of His Will, but you need to move.

    - Tell Him what you are going to do and ask Him to block it if it's not His Will.

Motivation of our lives

- God wants our new heart to be the motivation of our lives—He wants His Life in our hearts to determine all our choices.

- Loving God with all our heart means becoming one heart with Him and doing His Will from our heart.

Group Discussion Questions

1. Describe how we become *one heart* with God. (1 John 3:3-5; Ezekiel 11:19; Jeremiah 32:39; 1 John 5:12)

    When we make our initial choice to bind our hearts with God and become born again, we become one heart with Him. This is the time that God takes away our stony heart and gives us a brand new heart.

(Pages 175, 185-186)

2.   Loving God with all our heart means allowing God's Life in our heart to be the *motivation* for all we choose to do. Explain what this means. (Ephesians 6:6c; Romans 6:17b; 2 Corinthians 5:14a) Can you give some examples?

Loving God with all our heart means "...doing the will of God from our hearts." (Ephesians 6:6) It means allowing God's Life in our hearts to be the instigation for all we choose to do and not our self-life.

(Pages 175, 183, 187-188)

3.   Describe our heart and explain why it's such an important area. (Matthew 7:24-25; Proverbs 4:23b; 14:30a; Matthew 7:24-25)

Our heart life is the center core of our whole being. It's the essential nature and true essence of our whole person. Our heart is the place where our thoughts, emotions and desires are originally created, started and begun. The reason our heart is such an important area is that it's the foundation block upon which everything else is built.

(Pages 175, 185)

4.   What's the *purpose* for God's supernatural Life in our hearts? (Ephesians 5:17-18; John 7:38; John 4:14) What must occur *in us* for God's Life to come forth? (Romans 6:11-13) What happens if we choose not to do this? (Psalm 119:70a; Hebrews 3:13; Matthew 13:15). Give examples.

The purpose of God's Life in our hearts is to motivate us, fill us and then overflow us to others (just like a well of water). Then others will be able "to see" the real Jesus in us.

In order for this to occur, however, we must first choose to yield ourselves to God and reckon ourselves dead to sin. If we choose not to do this, we quench God's Spirit and stop His Life from flowing through us to others. Often this results in our becoming hardened and not hearing or understanding anything of God.

(Pages 159, 161, 175-176, 186)

5.   Define sin. (Isaiah 59:2; Romans 14:23c; 1 John 5:17a)

Sin is anything that causes us to be separated from God. Sin is anything that is not of faith. (Pages 178-179)

6.   Name some common sins we don't often recognize. What happens to God's Love when we sin?

Some common sins we often don't recognize are; self-pity, self-defensiveness, oversensitivity, criticalness, resentfulness, worry, grumbling, bossiness, self-energy, self-consciousness, etc.

If we are doing any of the above, God's Love in our hearts is blocked. Then, we not only won't experience His Love for others, but we also won't experience His Love for ourselves.

(Pages 161, 178, 185)

7.   Are all negative thoughts sin? Why/Why not? When do they become sin?

No, all negative thoughts are not sin. The original bad thought itself is not sin. The separation from God occurs when we choose to follow what that negative thought is prompting us to do, over what God is telling us to do. We sin even when we entertain, mull over, or bury bad thoughts, rather than give them to God.

(Page 178)

8.   Define pride. (Isaiah 14:13-14; 47:8)

Pride is following what we think, feel and want over what God wants. Pride is saying "I will" rather than "what God wills." Pride is not loving (agapao) God first, but self. (Page 179)

9.   In James 3:10-12, it describes the "pure water coming out bitter." What does this mean and why does this grieve God? (James 3:10b)

Bitter water here, I believe, refers to our "self-life." And fresh water is "God's Life." This Scripture is telling us that these two opposing things should not be coming forth from the same person. This is not God's plan. As James says, "this should not be." God wants His Life, and His Life alone, to be manifested from our lives.

(Pages 159, 161, 175-176)

10. Name the four types of hearts described in Luke 8:11-15. Briefly describe each one.

The four hearts are:

*   The unregenerate heart—a person who is not a believer because the Word of God has fallen, not in his heart, but, "by the wayside."

*   The hardened heart—a person, again an unbeliever, who hears the Word of God but, because he has no root (in his heart), he immediately falls away.

*   The sin-covered heart—a believer who refuses to deal with his sin, and thus, the Spirit in his heart is quenched and he bears no fruit.

*   The willing heart—a believer who has made faith choices and is thus, an open and cleansed vessel, ready and willing to do whatever God asks.

(Pages 179-180, 186-187)

11. How does understanding our brand-new heart help us in making godly choices?

    I believe visually seeing the effects (results) of sin in our lives (covering our hearts and preventing God's Love) should prompt and motivate us to confess, repent and give "anything that is not of faith" over to God, so that once again His Life can flow.

12. In review, loving God with all our heart means essentially two things. What are they? (Ezekiel 36:26; 1 John 5:12; Ephesians 6:6c; 2 Corinthians 5:14)

    Loving God with all our heart means:

    1) Asking Jesus into our hearts and becoming *one heart* with Him.

    2) Allowing His Life in our hearts to be the *motivation* for all we choose.

    (Pages 175, 183)

Personal Questions

1. Have you or are you experiencing any situations or struggles similar to those that were shared in this teaching? If so, what situations?

2. Which of the following tend to motivate your choices and actions? Circle those that apply to you)

fear	hurt	doubt	anger
anxiety	guilt	pride	bitterness
resentment	insecurities	negative thoughts	
defensiveness	need to control	other _____	

3. What happens when you choose to follow these thoughts? Next time this occurs, what Scriptures could you use to replace them?

   Suggested Scriptures: Psalm 51:2-3 and 1 John 1:9. (See *Survival Kit Prayer* at the end of Chapter 14 for more Scriptures.)

4. 1 Peter 4:2 tells us, we "no longer should live the rest of [our lives] to the lusts of men but to the **will of God**."

   Open discussion.

5. How can we know what the Will of God is? (Psalms 32:8; 119:9,105,130,169)

   We can know God's Will by reading His Word, by seeking competent counsel, by prayer and by watching what God does.

   (Pages 180, 181)

6. When you must make a decision and you're not certain of God's Will, what are the four things you should do?

   The four things we must do when we are not sure of God's Will are:

   • Pray and acknowledge God is in control.

- Tell Him you are not sure what His Will is, but you have to move.

- Tell Him what you are about to do.

- Ask Him to block it, if it is not His Will.

(Pages 181, 187)

7.   Are there any key points in this chapter that you are still struggling with or having difficulty with?

Open discussion.

Continue at Home

1.   Write on a note card all the Scriptures that particularly ministered to you in this chapter. Use them to help you apply these principles. Memorize them.

2.   Become aware of the negative thoughts that take away your peace. Note them in your journal. Confess them, repent of them, and then give them to God. Don't let them accumulate and separate you from God.

3.   Watch over your heart, as Scripture tells us, and let His Life in your heart be the *motivation* for all you choose to do this week.

4.   Ask God to help you recognize and deal with those "subtle sins" you often commit without even realizing it.

5.   Continue your exercise of seeing how long you can stay as Chart 5 (single-minded). When you slip and become Chart 6, how long does it take you to "clean up" and return to being Chart 5?

READ:
John 3
Galatians 5
Romans 6 and 7
James 3

Chapter 12: Loving God With All Our Willpower
DVD 3 - Session 5 - 38 minutes

Dianoia

- Greek word translated "mind" in the First Commandment.

- More properly translated it means willpower or volition.

Sh'ma (Deuteronomy 6:4-5)

- God did not ask Old Testament saints to love Him with all their will.

- God asks us to do this because we have the indwelling power of the Holy Spirit to enable us to live in obedience to God's Will.

- The Spirit of God is what gives us the power and authority to become one will with God.

The key to our Christian walk

- Our willpower is the authority and the power to choose God's Will regardless of what we think or feel.

- Our willpower enables us to put God's Life out into our souls.

- It's what determines whose life will be lived in our souls.

Our willpower has two parts

- God's supernatural Will and Power—where God counsels us as to what His Will is and then gives us the supernatural power to perform that Will in our lives.

- Our own free choice—where we have the authority and power to choose either God's Will and rely upon His Power to perform it in our lives, or choose our own will and rely upon our own ability to perform it.

Contrary choices

- This is a choice that goes against what we think, feel and desire.

- This is a faith choice or a non-feeling choice.

- Believers are the only ones who possess this supernatural ability to go against self—because we are the only ones who have a supernatural power within us to perform something different than what we feel or think.

- We don't have to "feel" our choices, we just need to be willing to make them.

God's authority and power

- Keys to the kingdom—to bind and to loose.

- To bind means to prohibit or forbid self—to loose means to permit or to allow self.

Exousia

- We have the choice to relinquish ourselves and do as God wants or to hold on to what we think and feel and do what we please.

- God is the one who gives us the authority to override our own feelings and the supernatural power to accomplish His Will in our lives.

Free Choice

- Only believers have free choice.

- Nonbelievers have a choice, but none of them have the authority to choose to go against how they really feel, because they don't have another power source within them to perform something different than what they think.

God changes our feelings

- After we have made faith choices, God is the one who aligns our feelings with our choices.

- We are not responsible to change our feelings—we are only responsible to make the right choice, putting God in charge.

- Often there is a period of time, before God aligns our feelings, where we must walk only by faith.

Healing is a process

- This process is made up of a million choices.

- The deeper the hurt, the longer the process takes to really "feel" the victory.

We have two kinds of choices

- Faith choices—choices free of emotion.

  - These are the only choices that unleash the power of God to come to our aid.

  - God's Life can then come forth from our hearts and be manifested in our souls.

  - This is being spirit-filled—or single-mindedness (living one life).

  - We are freed at this time from the power of sin.

  - Satan has no control of us—there are no holes

- Emotional choices—choices we make to follow our own thoughts, emotions, and desires over what God is prompting.

  - Power of sin is controlling us.

  - Self life is being manifest—our own thoughts, emotions, and desires (false witness).

  - God's Life is quenched and blocked—double-minded (two lives being lived).

  - Open to arrows of the enemy—many holes to attack.

Our choice is where sin begins

- The battle is either won or lost in the area of our willpower.

- It's not sin to have the original bad thought—it's what we choose to do with that thought that determines whether we sin or not.

- When we choose to entertain or follow that thought, it becomes sin.

We can't fix our self-life

- Self-life does not improve with age.

- Can't tame it, we must kill it.

- Maturity in Christ is simply recognizing our self-life and making the appropriate faith choices to give it to God.

Exchanging lives with Christ

- We must learn to set our self-life aside, so Jesus can live His Life through us.

- We give God our life, He then gives us His.

Loving God with all our willpower

- It means becoming one will with God.

- It's the key to our walking by the Spirit.

Group Discussion Questions

1. When we are born again, we receive a brand-new spirit and a brand-new heart. What else do we receive? (Hebrews 8:10; 10:16 *Be sure to check the Greek)

   When we are born again, we also receive a new supernatural willpower. Our new willpower gives us the authority and the power to choose God's Will even when we don't feel like it. Our willpower is the "*key*" to our whole Christian walk.

   (Pages 190-191)

2.   More precisely translated, what does the word mind (dianoia) in the First
     Commandment mean? (Matthew 22:37)

     Dianoia means willpower or volition. It's our will and the power to perform it. "Dia"
     means channel and "noia" means of the Spirit. Our willpower is the channel for
     God's Spirit to flow from our hearts out into our lives.

     (Pages 153-154, 189-190, 209-210)

3.   Why didn't God command the Old Testament saints to love Him with all their wills?
     (Deuteronomy 6:5; Galatians 4:6; 1 Corinthians 6:17)

     Jesus exhorts us New Testament believers to love Him with all our willpower
     because we have the indwelling Power of the Holy Spirit to do so. The Old
     Testament saints did not have the indwelling Power of God to perform His Will in
     their lives.

     (Pages 189-190)

4.   In this chapter we use the term "supernatural willpower." Summarize what this
     means. (Matthew 26:39d, 1 Peter 4:2; 1 Corinthians 7:37) Why are Christians the
     only ones who possess this supernatural willpower? (Romans 7:18)

     God's supernatural Willpower means that God will counsel us as to what His Will is
     and then give us the supernatural Power to perform that Will in our lives. In other
     words, Christians are the only ones who can make choices that go against what
     they think and feel, because they are the only ones who have another power
     source within them to perform something different than what they feel.

     (Pages 190-194)

5.   Describe the purpose of our willpower. (1 John 5:20; Ephesians 1:18-19—again,
     see Greek) What are the two parts of our willpower? (Philippians 2:13;
     Deuteronomy 30:19-20)

     The purpose of our willpower is to give us the authority and power to choose God's
     Will, even when we don't feel like or want to make that choice. This is why our
     willpower is the "*key*" to our Christian walk. It's what enables us to put God's Life
     from our hearts out into our lives (souls), regardless of how we feel.

     The two parts of our willpower are:

     •   God's supernatural Will and Power—where God counsels us as to what His
          Will is and then gives us the Power to perform it in our lives.

     •   Our free choice—where we have the freedom to follow what God has shown
          us and allow Him to perform it in our lives; or, the freedom to follow what our
          own thoughts and emotions are telling us and rely upon our own ability to
          perform that.

     (Pages 153-154, 190-191, 209-210)

6.   Define what is meant by *free choice*. (John 10:17-18) Do all people have free

choice? Why/Why not? (Ephesians 2:2-3; 4:17-19; Colossians 1:21)

Our free choice is the freedom to either follow what God has shown us and trust in His Power to perform that in our lives (i.e., make "faith choices"), or choose to do what we think and feel and trust in our own power to accomplish it in our lives.

We have a constant choice as to whom we will yield our members—either to God and His Will or to self and our own desires.

(Pages 153-156, 190-191, 193-195)

7. Why is our willpower so critical? (Jeremiah 21:8; Ephesians 1:18; 1 John 5:20— see Greek)

    Again, our willpower is critical because it's what enables us to put God's Life from our hearts out into our lives, regardless of how we feel.

    (Pages 190, 200)

8. Explain why our willpower is often described as "the keys to the kingdom." (Matthew 16:19; Isaiah 22:22; Revelation 3:7)

    Scripture tells us that the "keys to the kingdom" allow us to bind on earth and to loose in heaven.

    In the context we have been studying, to bind means "to prohibit or forbid self" and to loose means "to permit and to allow self."

    I believe Christians possess the authority and the power, through our supernatural willpower, to either make a faith choice (thus, forbidding self to rule) or make an emotional choice (thus, allowing self to reign).

    (Pages 193-195)

9. When we make a *faith choice*, can we know it was genuine by how we feel? Why/Why not? Describe some faith choices you have made in your life.

    Our feelings are never a good barometer for truth. Our feelings are usually just the opposite of what is true. As humans we are so programmed to "feel" all our choices. But as Christians this does not have to be the case. We have the supernatural authority (by our new willpower) to go against how we feel and have it still be genuine and true. God, then, is the One who changes our feelings to match our choices.

    (Pages 190-195)

    Solicit examples from group.

10. If we make the right faith choices, what happens to our *feelings* and our uncontrolled emotions? (Mark 9:24) Are we responsible to change our feelings? Who is? What is our responsibility? (Isaiah 1:19; Matthew 26:39; Luke 5:5)

    Praise God, if we can first of all, simply acknowledge and express our real feelings, confess and repent of them, and give them over to God. Then we can know that

God will be faithful (in His timing) to change our feelings to match our faith choices. We are not responsible to change our feelings. Our responsibility is to put in charge the only person who *can* change our feelings and that's God.

(Pages 191, 195)

11.   When we make faith choices, whose life is lived in our soul? Why is this called *single- mindedness*? Explain.

When we make faith choices, we'll be those cleansed vessels and God's Life will freely flow into our souls. His Love becomes our love—His Wisdom and Power, our own. This is called "single- mindedness" because only *one* life is being lived— God's. (See Chart 5.)

(Pages 159, 200)

12.   Scripture tells us that when we make *faith choices*, we are freed from sin. How does this work? (Romans 6:6-7; Galatians 5:24; John 14:30c) What else occurs? (Zechariah 4:6c; Luke 1:45)

When we make faith choices, we are freed from sin because our self-life has been set aside and prohibited. For that moment, there are no "holes" for Satan to grab hold of. Our uncontrolled thoughts are reined in; our wild emotions yielded, and our desires submitted. And God's Life is free, to flow from our hearts out into our lives. (See Chart 5.)

(Pages 159-200)

13.   What three things happen when we choose to follow our own thoughts, emotions and desires over what God is prompting us to do? (Luke 8:14; Romans 7:15, 19, 23; James 1:8; Proverbs 5:22; John 8:34; Isaiah 59:2) Give examples.

The three things that happen when we choose to follow our own thoughts are:

•   The power of sin controls us.

•   God's Spirit is quenched and His Love blocked.

•   God's eternal life cannot flow to others or to ourselves. (Pages 161, 178, 204)

14.   Why is Satan thrilled when we make emotional choices? (Joel 1:10,12; Luke 11:17; Jeremiah 7:28; Luke 8:14) Why is this called *double-mindedness*? (James 1:8)

Satan is happy when we make emotional choices because we immediately quench God's Spirit and Christ's Life is not passed on. This is double-mindedness because there are two lives being lived here. (See - Chart 6.)

(Pages 160-161, 204-205)

15.   Where does sin begin? (James 1:14-15; 4:17; Romans 14:23) What is the consequence of allowing sin to proceed? (Ephesians 4:19; 1 Corinthians 5:6-7; Lamentations 3:44; Galatians 5:19-21)

Any choice not to obey God is going to quench God's Spirit and separate us from Him. This causes the door of our hearts to close.

The first ungodly thought is not sin. The sin enters when we choose to follow what that negative thought is telling us to do. Even if we just entertain and mull over those ungodly thoughts, it still ends up sin (and separating us from Him). The consequence of entertaining negative thoughts is that God's Life will be blocked and unable to flow.

(Pages 205-206, 211)

Personal Questions

1. A choice that goes against what we naturally think, feel and want is called a **contrary choice**. (Mark 9:24; Matthew 26:39; Luke 5:5c) Give examples in your own life where you had to make choices that you didn't feel, but because you were a willing and open vessel, God performed miracles through you in spite of how you felt.

2. Are there any situations in your life right now where you are having difficulty making *contrary choices* because of the circumstances, the other person's reactions, or your own emotions?

   Open discussion.

3. What three things happen when we make faith choices or contrary choices? God's Love becomes **our love**; His Thoughts become **our thoughts**; and, His Will becomes **our will**.

   (Page 200)

4. The key to making contrary choices is, simply, to **be willing**. (Isaiah 1:19; Matthew 26:39; John 5:30b)

   (Pages 53, 200-201)

5. Maturity in Christ is simply:

   (Hebrews 5:14; 2 Corinthians 4:10-12; Galatians 2:20)

   Recognizing our self life and making the appropriate faith choices to cleanse ourselves of all that God shows us, so that His Life can come forth. (Hebrews 5:14; 2 Corinthians 4:10-12; Galatians 2:20)

6. Are there any other areas in your life right now where you may be able to apply this teaching?

   Open discussion.

7. Are there any key points in this chapter that you are still struggling with or having difficulty with? Explain.

   Open discussion.

Continue at Home

1. Write on a note card all the Scriptures that ministered to you in this chapter. Use them to help you apply these principles. Memorize them.

2. Ask God to make you aware of your choices this week. Ask Him to remind you when you should be making contrary choices.

3. In Matthew 26:39 Jesus said, "Not my will, but thine." Write down some of your own thoughts and emotions that God has had you surrender to Him this week. (Ephesians 4:31; Colossians 3:5-9; Hebrews 12:15) Did you recognize them immediately? Did you give them over to God right away? Explain.

4. Philippians 2:13 says that God is in us not only "to will," but also "to do." This week, continually pray for His Power to produce His Life in you. (2 Corinthians 4:11-12) Share the situations He gives you to practice this.

READ: MEMORIZE:
Romans 6 and 7   Mark 9:2
1 John 5:20
Philippians 2:13
Matthew 26:39
Luke 5:5

Chapter 13: Loving God With All Our Soul
DVD 3- Session 6 - 1 hr, 4 minutes

Faith choices are not enough

- We must also give God our lives to perform those choices through—it's a faith walk also.

- It's critical not to let our negative emotions accumulate.

What is our soul?

- Greek word for soul is psyche—which means "it shall have life" or "it shall wax cold."

- Our soul is a neutral area that will either be filled with God's Spirit and have life—or be filled with self-life and wax cold.

Our purpose as Christians

- To be filled with the fullness of God—filled with His Life (His Love, Wisdom and Power).

- Nothing will bring us greater joy and fulfillment.

God's Image

- An image is an exact likeness of something.

- If our soul is filled with God's Life, we will reflect His Image.

- His Image will be our identity.

Self image

- Reflecting what we think, feel and desire.

- God wants us to set that self aside and show forth His Image.

Healthy self image

- If we know God loves us:

- We will have the trust to lay down our wills and lives to God (and love Him).

- Then it will be His Life that comes forth through us.

- As a result, we will begin to like (storge) what we say and do. This is God-confidence and Christ- esteem.

Poor self image

- If we don't know God loves us:

  - We won't have the confidence to lay down our wills and lives to God and His Life will be quenched in our hearts.

  - Then it will be our own self-life that comes forth in our souls (not God's Life)—we'll be phonies, hypocrites.

- As a result, we won't like (storge) what we say or do, because it's not God through us as it should be.

Three areas of our soul

Conscious thoughts:

- Thoughts are most important—they begin the chain reaction of our souls (thoughts-emotions- desires-actions).

- We are not responsible for original negative thought—it's what we choose to do with it that causes sin and separates us from God.

- If we recognize the bad thought and give it to God—we have not sinned and are not separated from God.

We are not to grieve the Holy Spirit.

  - We are not to share things that don't edify.

  - If we do, we contaminate the other person and reprogram that thought back in again. This is the reason psychology can be so dangerous.

  - Here, we are not dealing with the sin, but mulling it over and trying to figure out our own corrupt thoughts.

  - God is the only one who can expose the hidden things of our soul—the true root causes.

- God's thoughts:

  - Come in that still, small voice.

  - Encourage peace.

  - Draw us closer to Him.

  - Are always in agreement with His Word.

  - Often must reprove us or convict us of sin—still, they will push us closer to Jesus not away from Him.

- Thoughts from the flesh:

  - Satan uses things of the flesh to cause us to sin.

- We must recognize these and deal with them immediately.

- These will go away pretty quickly.

- Satan's voice:

  - It's a loud, demanding voice.

  - It's a "do it now" thought—it causes unrest and doubt (condemnation).

  - It pushes us away from God.

- Satan's strongholds:

  - Are areas that we have given him previously—he won't give these up easily.

  - When our feelings don't align with our choices, Satan tries to make us think God is not faithful—it didn't work.

  - God lets us go awhile to strengthen us—He uses Satan as His tool to bring to light things that are hidden.

  - God wants us to give these things to Him and be free of them forever.

  - It's imperative to recognize the battle—use our weapons of warfare.

- Imagination:

  - Be aware of anything that causes us to dwell in our past—"how it used to be."

  - Prompts melancholy thoughts.

  - We must forget the things of the past—we don't have to figure or reason them out—we are not responsible for the sins of others.

Conscious emotions

- Our emotions are not spontaneous—they are a direct result of what we have allowed in our thought life.

- Some emotions are righteous—with no sin involved.

- Sinful emotions are those that are "not of faith."

  - Example: Depression is being consumed with negative thoughts that we are choosing not to deal with.

  - We must always confess our own responsibility in the sin—we have chosen to hang on to the negative thoughts rather than give them to God.

  - God is the one who will make us genuine.

Conscious desires

- Our own natural desires that are usually contrary to God's—these can become out-of-control lusts.

- We have God's authority to choose God's Will over our own.

- We don't have to "feel" these choices—just be willing to make them.

- Satan uses our lusts to revenge God—he gets back at God through us.

- God often gives us the desires of our hearts after we have laid them at His feet.

Our souls are like our feet

- Our souls get dirty.

- We don't need to take a complete bath, only to recognize our wrong choices and be cleansed from them.

Loving God with all our soul

- It's relinquishing our self-life so that God's Life can come forth from our hearts.

- It's becoming one life with God—exchanging my life for His.

Group Discussion Questions

1. Describe the difference between our soul and our heart (Proverbs 4:23; Isaiah 58:11)

   Our heart is the place where God's Life is created and brought into new existence by God's Holy Spirit. Our new heart life is God's supernatural Love, Wisdom and Power. It's invisible life (hidden life). Our souls are made up of our thoughts, emotions and desires (conscious and unconscious). Our souls are mainly the outward expression of our lives—or visible life. Our soul is a neutral area that is either going to be Spirit-filled (filled with God's Life) or filled with self-life.

   (Pages 148-150, 156-162, 215-216)

2. Define our purpose as Christians. (1 John 4:7-8; Philippians 1:21; Ephesians 3:19; 2 Corinthians 4:10-11)

   Our whole purpose as Christians is to be filled with God's Life; sharing His genuine Love with others; manifesting His Life, not our own; glorifying Him and being conformed into His Image.

   (Pages 33, 159, 216-217)

3. What determines whose life will be lived in our souls? (Isaiah 59:2)

   Our choices (our willpower) is what determines whose life will be lived in our souls. It's the "key" to our Christian walk.

   If we choose to hold on to sin (by making emotional choices), then God's Life will be quenched in our hearts and our self-life will be manifested.

   (Pages 159, 190, 204-206)

4.   We must do more than make the right *faith choice*. What other step of faith must we take in order for it to genuinely be God's Life flowing through us? (Romans 12:1; Galatians 5:25)

We must not only make the right faith choices, but we must also lay down our lives so that God can perform His Will through them. We must present our bodies as living sacrifices and believe that God will be faithful to do, through us, what He says.

(Pages 213-215)

5.   Loving God with all our soul means "exchanging our own self-image for the image we were created to bear, which is Christ's Image." Explain what this means. (Romans 8:29; 1 John 4:17; Colossians 3:10) Give some examples.

God wants us to set aside all our own thoughts, emotions and desires that are contrary to His (our self-life) and to be filled with His Life from our hearts. If we give God "our life," He then gives us His, and we'll be able to shine forth His Image (His Likeness) to others.

(Pages 217-218)

6.   How is it that we are able to exchange our life for God's? (John 12:24-25; 1 Corinthians 15:31b; Matthew 26:39)

It's only as we learn to love God (to totally give ourselves over to Him) that His Life, already in our hearts, can come forth. Only as we yield, surrender and relinquish our self-life to God are we able to be filled with His Life.

(Pages 115, 158-159, 213)

7.   Define "identity." Give the four steps in building a healthy identity. (Isaiah 43:4; Luke 9:23-24; Philippians 1:21; 1 John 4:17)

Our identity is who we think and feel ourselves to be. The four steps in building a healthy identity are:

1)   Knowing God loves us.

2)   Laying down our wills and our lives to Him.

3)   God's Life will then be freed to come forth.

4)   We'll then "like" what we say and what we do (because it's God's Life through us). (Pages 219-220)

8.   Why does our confidence soar when we are "filled with God?" (2 Corinthians 3:5; 4:6-7) What happens when we refuse to allow God to conform us into His Image?

(Ephesians 4:17-20; Romans 1:21-25, 29; John 5:31)

Our confidence soars when it's God's Life coming forth through us, because we'll "like" what we do and what we say. When we refuse to be conformed into His Image however, we won't be pleased with what we do or what we say, because it won't be God's Life through us as it should be, but our own self-life.

(Pages 219-220)

9. Summarize what it is that causes us to have a poor self-image. (Jeremiah 5:25; Ezekiel 16:15; Romans 9:20; Matthew 23:25-27; Romans 7:15, 19) Why does this occur even after we are Christians? (Isaiah 29:13; Romans 7:19-20) Give examples.

    The following are the reasons we have a poor self image:

    1) We don't know God loves us.

    2) Therefore, we don't have the confidence to lay our wills and our lives down to Him (and love Him).

    3)   God's Life in our hearts becomes quenched (covered) because of sin.

    4) Thus, we won't like the life that comes forth from us, because it's not God's Life, but our own.

    This pattern occurs even after we are Christians, because we continue to make emotional choices that block and quench God's Life in our hearts.

    (Pages 160-162, 204-205, 220)

10. Name the three areas of our soul. Explain the "chain reaction" that occurs in our souls each time we choose to act.

    The three areas of our soul are: our conscious and subconscious thoughts, emotions and desires.

    Our thoughts are the most important area of our soul because they are the first to be triggered in the chain reaction of our soul. Our thoughts stir up our emotions; our emotions influence our desires; and our desires produce our actions.

    (Pages 221-222, 239-240)

11. Explain why are our thoughts are so important. Why must we learn to "take every thought captive"? (2 Corinthians 10:5-6; 2 Samuel 11:2-4)

    Our thoughts are critical because they are the first to be triggered in the chain reaction of our souls. If we can catch our negative thoughts when they first occur, we can stop the chain reaction altogether.

    Our thoughts are important because we always think before we feel. If we "take every thought captive," then we can stop the sin before it ever begins and continue to reflect God.

    (Pages 221-222, 239-240)

12. Are we responsible for our initial negative (bad) thought? Why/Why not? What can we do the next time we have negative thoughts?

No, we are not responsible for the original negative thought. It's what we choose to do with that negative (bad) thought that makes it sin or not. Even if we do nothing with it, it will eventually be programmed in and become sin.

The next time we have a bad thought, we must "deal with it" by:

1)   Recognizing it.

2)   Confessing it.

3)   Giving it to God.

4)   And replacing it with God's Word. (Pages 222-223, Chapter 14)

13. Is it wrong for a Christian to acknowledge his negative (bad) thoughts and feelings to himself and to God? Explain. What are the three ways we can "deal with" our negative thoughts and feelings as God would have us? What are we enabling Satan to do when we choose *not* to deal with these things? (Proverbs 5:22; John 8:34)

No, it's not wrong to acknowledge our negative thoughts. God wants us to acknowledge what we are thinking and feeling, so we can know exactly what to give over to Him.

God would have us:

1) Catch the negative thoughts as they come in.

2) Refuse them.

3) And give them over to God.

We enable Satan to build strongholds in our hidden chambers if we entertain, mull over or hold on to bad thoughts.

(Pages 222-228, 248-250)

14. How can we tell the difference between God's voice, Satan's voice, and our own? What does the term "strongholds of the enemy" mean and why are these strongholds harder to get rid of? (Proverbs 5:22; John 8:34)

God's voice is a still, small voice prompting peace, encouragement, and always a closer walk with Him. His voice is always in agreement with His Word.

The urgings of our flesh (jealousy, bitterness, etc.) often push us to sin, but if we are faithful to confess, repent and give these things to God, they will most likely go away.

Satan's voice is a very loud, shrill and demanding voice. It's an urgent "do it now" kind of thought. These are the thoughts that cause doubt and unrest. Satan's voice condemns us, makes us feel guilty, and always pushes us away from God.

"Strongholds of the enemy" are things that Satan is involved in and these are negative thoughts and emotions that often do come back and back again. Satan has used these as "hideouts" and he's not going to give them up easily. We have allowed him room there (ground) by holding on to these things and not giving them over to God.

(Pages 224-227, 239)

15. What happens when we "share" and "re-hash" our negative (bad) thoughts with others? (Ephesians 4:29-30; Isaiah 3:24a) What happens when we "dwell on" or try to "figure out" our past? What does God want us to do with our negative thoughts and past experiences? (Psalm 103:12; Galatians 5:24; Philippians 3:13b; Isaiah 43:18-19)

When we share our ungodly thoughts with others, we not only contaminate them, but we also automatically reprogram those negative thoughts right back down inside. Thus, our emotions become stirred up all over again.

When we dwell on our past (as in psychology), we continually focus on the negative things about ourselves and others and we reprogram those things back in our subconscious—again, creating even more strongholds.

God wants us to take every thought captive and "deal with it" recognizing it; confessing it; and repenting of it (refusing to even let it go in); and finally, giving it to God (crucifying it).

(Pages 223-224)

16. 2 Corinthians 10:3-6 talks about our "weapons of warfare." What are they and where is the battle waged?

God's weapons of warfare are His Word, His Blood and His Name.

The battle between the Spirit and the flesh is won or lost in the area of our willpower. Our "choice" to follow what the negative thoughts are telling us, is where sin begins. (Pages 205-206, 225-226)

Personal Questions

1. According to these Scriptures, what blessings do we receive from loving God with all our soul?

Luke 18:29-30 (We will receive 100 times more in the present time, all we have chosen to set aside, and in the world to come, life everlasting).

John 14:27 (Don't let your heart be troubled, peace I leave you). John 15:11 (Your joy might be full).

John 15:11 (Your joy might be full).

John 8:36 and 2 Corinthians 3:17 (You shall be free and have liberty). John 14:14 (Ask anything in His Name, we will receive it).

Romans 6:22-23 (Freed from sin, servants of God, fruit unto holiness). Romans 8:38-39 (Nothing will separate us from His Love).

John 8:36 and 2 Corinthians 3:17 (You shall be free and have liberty).

Galatians 5:22-23 (All the fruit of the Spirit).

Ephesians 1:18-19 (Eyes of your understanding will be opened to know—Hope of His calling, riches of the glory of His inheritance, and greatness of His Power).

James 1:12 (Receive a crown of Life).

2. Can you think of an example in your own life where you made the right faith choice, but forgot to lay down your life so God could perform His Will through you? What happened?

    Open discussion.

    See example in Chapter 13, "The Hated Stepmother."

3. When you have difficulty laying down your life to God, what is the one basic fact you must always remember? (Isaiah 43:1-4; Matthew 10:29-31)

    The basic fact that we must always remember is that God loves us and will never leave us nor forsake us. If we know that He loves us, then we'll have confidence to continually lay down our wills and lives and love Him in return.

    (Pages 91-92, 242-243)

4. Is there anything in your life right now that you are afraid to lay down before God? If so, what is it and why are you afraid?

    Open discussion.

5. Consider if there is any area in your life right now where you have been trying to "improve yourself," rather than simply *exchanging lives* with God. Explain.

    Open discussion.

    Ask questions like:

    *   In what areas are you "trying to be" more loving, less self-centered, etc.?

    *   Are you sure it's God doing these things through you or is it you trying to "fix up" your- self?

    The key is "emptying yourself" first, so that you can be filled with God. (Pages 206-207)

Continue at Home

1. Ask God to show you any lies about yourself that you have programmed in over the years, and upon which you are basing your identity. Choose to give these over to God and replace them with His truth. (See the "Who I Am in Christ" Scriptures in the Supplemental Study Notes found in this book.)

2. Share a situation where you had no love for another person, and you had to be that "open vessel" so God could love them through you. What happened?

READ: MEMORIZE:
John 13:7-10   Galatians 5:25
Colossians 1 and 3   Philippians 1:21
Ephesians 4   1 John 4:17
2 Corinthians 4   Mark 10:29-30

Chapter 14: Eight Steps to Survival
DVD 4 - Session 7- 1 hr, 12 minutes

Survival Kit

- Steps God has laid out for us in Scripture to help us deal with our sin and become open and cleansed vessels for His use.

- First four steps are formalities—we don't have to do these each time we sin.

- Last four steps (Inner Court Ritual) are mandatory—we must do these each time we sin and quench God's Spirit.

Attitudes we must have

- Presenting our bodies as living sacrifices.

  - Don't have to "feel" each of these steps.

  - We must remember God loves us unconditionally—and that He is faithful.

  - He will not allow anything to happen in our lives that is not "Father-filtered."

- Continually denying ourselves—our "justified" thoughts and feelings.

  - Being willing to lay everything down at His feet.

  - All Christians are capable of doing this, but not all Christians are willing to do this--if we are, God says He will return to us a hundredfold.

- Be willing to do God's Will no matter what—getting up and doing what God has called us to do.

- Be willing to take every thought captive.

  - Capture ungodly thoughts first—stop the chain reaction of our souls.

  - If we don't take those thoughts captive, they will take us captive.

Four mandatory steps

- Recognize ungodly thoughts, emotions and desires.

  - Ask God to expose the truth and shed light on our hidden chambers.

  - We need to "see" not only the surface emotions, but also the root causes of these emotions.

  - Get alone with God—He is only one who can expose, cleanse and totally heal us.

  - We must be cleansed in order to respond correctly.

- Don't confront another unless you are cleansed.

- We must acknowledge and experience our real feelings—call them by name—be honest.

- Expressing our real self-life is part of the cleansing process—we must recognize real feelings before we can give them over to God.

- We have three choices of what to do with our thoughts:

- Vent them, stuff them, or give them to God and be rid of them forever.

- Give them to God or they will motivate all our actions.

- Confess and repent of all the Holy Spirit shows us and unconditionally forgive anyone who has wronged us (Lavers of Bronze).

  - Confess and repent of anything that has separated us from God.

  - This is our own responsibility—we must acknowledge whatever we have done.

  - We must also receive God's forgiveness for ourselves.

- Give over to God all He has shown us that is not of faith (Holocaust Altar).

  - Give not only the symptoms, but also the root causes.

  - The root cause is often a stronghold of the enemy.

  - Give as "love gifts," with no strings attached.

- Read God's Word (Molten Sea).

  - Replace the lies with the truth.

  - Only God, by His Word, can cleanse, heal and sanctify us completely.

  - Memorize Scriptures.

  - Praise God—He will work all things together for good!

Be an example

- Be open and frank with your spouse and children.

- Keep a journal.

Loving God is

- Continually relinquishing our wills and lives to Him.

- Becoming one heart, will and life with Him—so that all that is seen through us is Him.

- This is the marriage relationship He desires.

Group Discussion Questions

1. What are the four attitudes we must constantly have in order to love the Lord in the way He desires? (Romans 12:1-2; Philippians 3:8-15; Philippians 2:5; 2 Corinthians 10:5-6) Do we need to "feel" each of these attitudes? Why/Why not? (Romans 1:17)

   The four attitudes we must have are:

   1) Presenting our bodies as living sacrifices—giving God permission to expose what He wants.

   2) Continually denying ourselves and being willing to lay everything down to God.

   3) Being willing to get up and do what God asks—obeying His Will.

   4) Taking every thought captive and revenging all disobedience.

   We don't need to "feel" willing or want to make these choices, we simply must "be" willing. God then will change our feelings to match our choice.

   (Pages 195, 242-247, 265)

2. Romans 12:1 tells us we are to "present [our] bodies [as] a living sacrifice." What does this mean to you? (Job 13:15; 2 Corinthians 7:1; 2 Timothy 2:21)

   Presenting our bodies as living sacrifices means willingly giving God permission to expose all that He wants to in us—things He wants us to deal with.

   (Pages 242, 265)

3. When we talk about "denying ourselves," what exactly do we mean? (Philippians 3:8-15; John 12:24; Colossians 3:5,8-9) Are *all* Christians capable of denying themselves and "laying everything down?" If so, then why aren't more of us doing so?

   Denying ourselves means relinquishing and setting aside our own thoughts, emotions and desires that are contrary to God's so that His Life from our hearts can come forth. We must constantly ask ourselves, "are we more concerned about doing God's Will in our lives or our own happiness?"

   I believe all Christians are capable of laying everything down (because God is in them), but not all Christians are willing to do so.

   (Pages 243-244, 265)

4. Summarize why is it so important to "take every thought captive." (2 Corinthians 10:5-6) Is the first bad thought sin? Why/Why not? (2 Samuel 11:2-4)

   It's important to take every thought captive because our thoughts are the first to be triggered in the chain reaction of our souls. If we can catch our negative thoughts, then we prevent the whole chain reaction before it even begins. If we don't take every thought captive, we'll end up going along with the "tide of emotion" and end up separated from God (Isaiah 59:2). If we don't take the negative thoughts captive, they take us captive.

Remember, the original bad thought is not sin; it's what we choose to do with it that makes it sin or not.

(Pages 221-223, 246-247, 265)

5.   What are the four *mandatory* steps (the Inner Court Ritual) that the Old Testament has laid out for us? (Proverbs 20:27; 2 Corinthians 13:5; Job 12:22; Proverbs 1:23; 1 John 1:9; Acts 8:22; Matthew 6:14-15; Colossians 3:5,8; Ephesians 5:26; John 15:3)

The four mandatory steps we must take are:

1)   Recognizing our self-centered thoughts, emotions and desires. Asking God to expose our inner man and acknowledging how we feel (i.e., experiencing our emotions).

2)   Confessing and repenting of all that God shows us and unconditionally forgiving anyone who has wronged us.

3)   Giving over to God (as love-gifts) all that He has shown us that is not of faith.

4)   Reading God's Word and replacing the lies with God's truth. It's important also to memorize God's Word.

(Pages 247-257, 263-266)

6.   Why is it so important to ask God to expose the "root cause" of our thoughts and feelings? (Proverbs 5:22; Job 12:22) Why do we need to "see" these buried things? (Psalm 139:23-24)

It's important to be cleansed in order to respond the way God would have us. Therefore, it's important to ask God to expose the "real" root cause of our conscious thoughts and emotions. If we can see and understand the root causes, then we'll know exactly what to give over to the Lord and those symptoms (hurtful thoughts and emotions) won't come back again.

(Pages 249-252)

7.   Do the things we push down in our hidden chambers stay there, or do they affect our lives in some way? What do we enable Satan to do when we don't deal with these negative things? (Proverbs 5:22; John 8:34)

It's impossible to hang onto negative thoughts and feelings without eventually acting out of them. These things automatically become the motivation for all of our actions. When we hang on to negative thoughts and feelings, we give Satan a perfect stronghold (hideout) to control our lives.

(Pages 225-228, 251-252)

8.   Define *confession* and *repentance*. (Isaiah 1:16; Ezekiel 18:30; 1 John 1:9)

Confession is acknowledging that what we have done is wrong. Repentance is simply changing our minds about following that sin (turning around) and instead choosing to follow God and what He wants us to do.

(Pages 252-253, 265-266)

9.   If someone has offended us, do we wait to forgive him until he comes to us and asks? (Matthew 6:14-15; 18:32-35; Colossians 3:13) What if we are "justified" feeling the way we do?

If we wait to forgive that other person until he asks for forgiveness, we might wait for years. God commands us to unconditionally forgive others their sin, even if we are justified by the world's standards. God is hindered from working in us or on the other party until we have "released" them. And we do that by unconditionally forgiving them.

(Pages 253-254, 266)

10. In your own words, what does it mean to *give over to God* (sacrifice) all that He has shown us about ourselves? (Luke 11:39-40; 1 Peter 5:7; Ephesians 5:2; 2 Timothy 2:21) Give examples.

God wants us to give Him anything that is "not of faith." Not only our conscious self-centered, bad thoughts, but also the subconscious (root) causes that God reveals to us.

(Pages 246-247, 251-252, 254-256)

11. Who is responsible for changing our feelings? Can't we just pray hard and change our own feelings? Explain why or why not.

We are not responsible for changing our own negative feelings. We are only responsible for put- ting in charge the only One who can change our feelings, and that's God.

In our own strength we can't fix or change our bad feelings. They are inside us and only Jesus (who made us) can change them. However, He has given us the authority and power to make "faith choices" (contrary choices) and in His timing, He will then align our feelings with those choices.

(Pages 190-191, 193-199, 252-253)

12. Why is it so important to "get into the Word" after we have given everything over (sacrificed) to the Lord? Explain. (Luke 11:24-26; Ephesians 5:26; John 15:3; James 1:21)

After we have given over to God all our hurts and emotions, we are still emotionally "bloody." At this point we need something that will soothe us, cleanse us, and totally heal us. Only the Word of God can do that.

(Pages 256-257)

Personal Questions

1.   What do you "naturally" tend to do with your negative thoughts and feelings? (2 Corinthians 13:5) Give examples. What does God desire you to do? Are you willing? Write out the Inner Court Ritual for yourself.

     Naturally, many of us seem to stuff our emotions. See example in Chapter 2, "Cold as Ice."

     God wants us to give all our sin to Him as "love gifts" (Luke 11:39-41) with no strings attached. We do this by:

     •   Recognizing and acknowledging our sins.

     •   Confessing and repenting of them.

     •   Giving them to God.

     •   Getting into His Word.

     (Pages 29, 260-261, 263-265, 268-269, 376) (Pages 27, 254-256, 258-260, 263-264, 369)

2.   Describe what specific self-centered thoughts, emotions, and desires get in your way of loving others with God's Agape Love. Write these down and then give them to God by going through the Inner Court Ritual.

     Emotions that often get in the way of our loving others are: criticalness, oversensitivity, self-consciousness, self-pity, etc.

     (Page 178)

3.   Think of a person who triggers ungodly reactions in you. Pray and ask God to show you *the root* cause of these feelings. When God shows you, go through the Inner Court Ritual and give them to God. (Psalm 139:22-24)

     Open discussion.

4.   Pray and ask God to show you other things you've been stuffing down in your hidden chambers. Deal with these things and, by faith, believe that God has cleansed you. Don't allow these things to come back by again thinking and meditating on them.

     Open discussion.

5.   Why is it so important to have a consistent quiet time and to be in the Word daily? (2 Thessalonians 2:15; Proverbs 8:34-35; James 1:5-6; Matthew 7:24; Psalm 32:8; 119:105)

     It's in our quiet time before the Lord that we daily go through the Inner Court Ritual so we can stay cleansed vessels. This is critical to do, so that we are "ready and prepared" to handle whatever God allows next. If we don't do this, we'll contaminate those we come in contact with.

(Pages 241-242, 259-260)

6.   Write out five Scriptures that particularly ministered to you from this chapter and use them to help you apply these principles.

Continue at Home

1.   Start using the <u>Survival Kit Prayer</u> found in the back of Chapter 14. If this one does not suit you, write your own. Also write out on 3x5 cards the *mandatory steps* to take when God's Spirit is quenched. Keep these cards with you at all times. You will need them when you are away from your notebook and Bible.

2.   Write a love letter to God and give Him all your hurts, anger, un-forgiveness, etc. Go through the Inner Court Ritual. Remember He loves you and wants to wash all these things away by His blood. He wants to free you. Ask Him to reveal any areas of pride, unbelief, or other strongholds of the enemy. Allow Him to do so.

3.   Ask God to make you more aware this week of any negative thoughts you might have toward others. Choose immediately to give these thoughts over to God (go through the four steps). Begin to make the Inner Court Ritual a *habit* in your life.

4.   Simply be aware of anything that takes your peace away. Ask God to show you specifically what's quenching His Spirit and separating you. Note in your journal the things He tells you and the things you give over to Him. Note, also, the Scriptures He gives you to replace the lies and untruths.

READ: MEMORIZE:
James 4   Psalm 119:9
Romans 6 and 7   1 John 1:9
Philippians 2 and 3   2 Corinthians 10:5

Chapter 15: Loving Others as Ourselves
Session 8 - DVD 4 -38 minutes

First and Second Commandments

- The two Great Commandments must go hand in hand and in the order they were given.

- We cannot love others (totally give ourselves over to them) until we have *first* loved God (totally given ourselves over to Him).

Loving others as ourselves is a *new* commandment

- It's only since Jesus gave us the indwelling Spirit that we have the authority and power to set ourselves aside and love others as ourselves.

- Old Testament saints did not have this supernatural ability—the Spirit of God came alongside, helping them and guiding them, but He never indwelt them (so they didn't have God's Love to give).

- In today's world, unbelievers and Christians who are not willing to lay down their wills and lives also do not have God's unconditional Love to give to others.

    - It's only when we relinquish our self-life that God's Love is allowed to flow through us.

    - We are to love as Jesus did—He died for us.

What does the Second Commandment really say?

- If we are loving God first, He then will enable us to love others *before or instead of* ourselves—un- conditionally give ourselves over to them.

- This is our mission and purpose as Christians—being full of God's Life to give to others.

Genuinely loving others (agapao) is naturally impossible

- Automatically we love (agapao) ourselves first.

- Intuitively we give ourselves over to our own will and desires before others.

- We don't have to be taught to do this—we are naturally self-centered (either pridefully or in a self-pity way).

- This is what God is trying to change in all of us.

Are we ever to love ourselves?

- Jesus is our example—there are no Scriptures that say He loved (agapao) Himself.

- What happened was:

  - The Father loved Jesus.

  - Jesus accepted that Love into His Life.

  - He then became the vessel to pass on that Love to us.

- This is the exact pattern God wants for us—to lay down our wills and lives so that we can be that open conduit for His Love to flow forth to others.

- So there is no need to ever love ourselves, because God has already done that.

Confusion over loving ourselves occurs

- Because it's fueled by the enemy to reinforce the root problem—more self-centeredness.

- Because most of us don't know the difference between the commitment love (agapao) and the affection love (storge).

Basic problem is

- Not that we don't love (agapao) ourselves (we do that naturally)—the problem is that we don't like (storge) ourselves.

- We don't know God loves us—thus we don't have confidence to lay our will and life down—thus it's not God's Life coming forth—thus we don't like what we say or what we do.

- Therefore, we never agapao self—we are to agapao God and others, and as a result we will like ourselves.

Extensions of God's Love

- God wants to pass His Love on through us—we are His arms and legs.

- Today God's Love has been quenched—the cross has been forgotten in our lives.

Things we can do to love others

- Love in action.

  - Our words and deeds must match, otherwise we are hypocrites.

  - Deeds of real Love are ones God motivates in our hearts and we do out of His Love, not out of duty.

  - These things are done out of a pure heart, not a clogged one.

- Comfort the fainthearted.

  - Share others' burdens.

  - Listen to one another—we don't have to have all the answers, especially if we have not been there.

  - Be genuine and real—transparency with God will allow us to be real and genuine with others.

  - Be vulnerable—not perfect (perfect people are not touchable).

  - Be honest—it will cause the masks of others to come down.

  - Self-life wants to hide the truth—God's Life wants to expose it.

  - Be humble—be willing to admit our own failures and needs.

- Be supersensitive to others' needs.

  - Set our own hurts aside and allow God to use us to minister to someone else in need.

  - Initiate God's Love to someone.

  - Pray for others, call, visit, or write them—be doers of His Word.

- Don't judge one another.

  - Don't question why God leads you somewhere or to someone.

  - Be an open channel for His Love—He will then accomplish His own purposes.

- They will know we are Christians by our Love.

  - By loving God, He will enable us to respond the way He desires.

  - Our Love for each other is proof we are loving Him.

Group Discussion Questions

1. In review, what does *agapao* mean? Who are we to love (agapao)? (1 Peter 1:22; 1 John 4:21; John 15:12-13; Matthew 22:37-39)

    Agapao means to totally give ourselves over to something; to be consumed with it; and to be completely committed to it. It's what we put first in our lives. It's a commitment love. This is the kind of love we are to love God and others with.

    (Pages 110-111, 269-271)

2. In Leviticus 19:18, God tells us to love one another. In the New Testament (John 13:34), however, Jesus calls "loving one another" a new commandment. Why is this now a new commandment?

    "Loving others" is now called a *new* commandment, because it's only since Jesus gave us the indwelling Power of His Spirit at our new birth that we can set aside our will and our lives in order to first "agapao" God and then others. This would not have been possible before the Spirit of God came to dwell in our hearts.

(Pages 270-271)

3.   How is it possible to love others *before or instead of* ourselves? (Matthew 22:37; 2 Corinthians 8:5: John 12:24; John 15:13; Philippians 2:5-9) Give examples.

When we first love God, He enables us to be that open vessel of His Love where it is possible to love others before, or instead of, ourselves. Because it's God's Love, we can unconditionally give ourselves over to others and be genuinely concerned about their will and desire *before* our own.

(Pages 271-272)

See example in Chapter 12, "I Love You More Than the Carpeting." and "Did You Tell Him Off?"

4.   John 13:34 tells us that Jesus is our example. How did Jesus love others? (John 15:9-17; 1 John 4:19; Matthew 20:28)

Jesus loved us so much, He died for us. He gave up everything for us—His rights, His will, His desires, His Life. Jesus not only loved His friends this way, He loved (agapao) His enemies this same way. (Luke 6:27-28)

(Pages 271-272, 296)

5.   Why don't we see the Christian Body today loving like Jesus did? (Matthew 24:12) Why is God's Love growing cold in our hearts?

True Agape Love, the genuine, self-sacrificing Love that Jesus talks about in the Bible is naturally and humanly impossible. The reason is that we love ourselves first, even after being born again. We automatically and instinctively give ourselves over to our own will and desires, (See Chart 6). It's only as we learn how to love God (die to self) that God's Agape Love will be released. Many Christians are not willing to do this. Thus, God's Love in their hearts is growing cold. The cross has been forgotten by much of the Christian body today.

(Pages 271-273, 275-276)

6.   What is the most important way that others will know we are true Christians? (John 13:35; 1 John 3:10, 14; 4:7-8,20) Give Scriptural examples.

The only way Scripture says others will know that we are Christians is by our Love (Agape Love for one another). Only Jesus' Love through us will bring our spouses, our bosses, and our families to God.

(Pages 58-60, 275-276)

7. Explain why we need to set ourselves aside and become open vessels before we can love others as ourselves. (2 Corinthians 4:10-12; John 15:13; Philippians 2:5-9)

    God's Love is passed on through us. He just needs an open and cleansed vessel so He can love His Love through us. This is the whole meaning and purpose of our lives.

    (Pages 57-58, 275)

8. Is it "natural" for us to love in the way that God desires? (Ephesians 5:29; Isaiah 47:8)

    It's totally impossible and unnatural to love the way God desires—unconditionally giving ourselves over to another. The only way this works is to love God first—choose to set ourselves aside (by the power of the indwelling Spirit) and become an open vessel. God can then fill us with His Love and enable us to love others before or instead of ourselves.

    (Pages 271-272)

9. Do we need to love ourselves first in order for us to love others? Why/Why not? (Ephesians 5:29; Philippians 2:21) Are we *never* to love (agapao) ourselves? (Isaiah 47:8)

    Absolutely not. We are never to completely give ourselves over to our own thoughts, emotions and desires before God or others. This is the root problem to begin with and what God is trying to change in all of us. We are never to "agapao" ourselves, only God and others.

    (Pages 272-273)

10. Describe the two primary ways we *naturally* love (are consumed with) ourselves. Give examples.

    The two primary ways we love (agapao) ourselves:

    1) Many of us are totally consumed with ourselves in a prideful, arrogant and boastful way.

    2) Others of us are just as much consumed with ourselves through self-hate and self-pity.

    Both ways are wrong, because both ways are consumed in and with ourselves before God and others.

    (Pages 271-272)

11. Why is there so much confusion in this area of "loving ourselves"? What is the root problem that God wants changed in each of us? (Philippians 2:21; Isaiah 47:8)

    The confusion over loving others occurs because of two major things:

    1) The confusion in the area of loving others is fueled by the enemy who, when

we are not having victory in our Christian walks, comes along and says "Well, the problem is you can't love others until you first love yourself." Because we see no other solution, we believe him.

2)   The second reason there is confusion in this area is that many of us don't know the difference between the natural, human, feeling loves (storge and phileo), and agapao, the commitment love.

This confusion then reinforces and strengthens the "root problem" in all of us—more self-centeredness—and we become more consumed in and with ourselves than ever before.

(Pages 272-273)

12.   How does God desire His cycle of Love to work? (1 John 4:10-12; 3:16; John 17:26)

God's "cycle of Love" works this way: The Father loved Jesus with Agape Love; Jesus accepted that Love of the Father into His Life. He then became the vessel to pass on that Love to others. This is the exact pattern God wants for each of our lives.

(Pages 272-273)

13.   What gives us a healthy self-identity so we can go on and love God and others the way He desires? Explain the difference between *Christ-esteem and God-confidence* and self-esteem and self-confidence. (Isaiah 30:15; Proverbs 3:26; 14:26)

The only way we can have a healthy self-identity is to know that God loves us. Then we can trustingly lay our wills and lives down to Him (as open and cleansed vessels). His Life from our hearts is then free to flow through us to others. As a result, we'll begin to "*like*" what we say and do because it's God's Life coming forth through us and not our own (see Chart 5). This is Christ- esteem and God-confidence.

If, however, we don't know that God loves us and we're not able to love Him in return, then it will be "self-life" that's shown forth through us (see Chart 6). This is where self-esteem and self- confidence comes from.

(Pages 158-162, 219-220, 274)

14.   Name four practical ways we can love others. (1 John 3:18; 2 Corinthians 1:3-4; Philippians 2:3; Romans 14:13) Give examples.

Four practical ways we can love others are:

1)   We can love others in action, not just with our words. (See example in Chapter 2, "Burnt Roast.")

2)   We can love others by comforting and encouraging them—by listening to them and then helping them carry their burdens to Jesus. (See example in Chapter

15, "We'll be Right Over," and "We're Going To Get a Divorce.")

    3)   We can love others by being supersensitive to their needs and by initiating God's Love. (See example in Chapter 15, "Backslidden For Three Years.")

    4)   We can love each other by not judging one another. (See example in Chapter 15, "You Are Not To Judge.")

(Pages 276-278, 284-285, 288-289, 293-294)

15.   Describe the secret to being real and genuine with others.

The secret to being real with others is by being transparent to God first. This is the key to allowing us to be genuine with others. It's having time alone with God so He can expose all that needs to be "dealt with" in us and we can continue to stay an open and cleansed vessel.

(Pages 249, 278-279)

16.   It's so difficult for us not to judge by appearance. What does Luke 16:15 have to say about this? Who is the only One to judge our hearts?

We all "naturally" walk by sight rather than by faith. It's natural for us to make judgments according to appearance, mannerisms, etc., rather than to depend upon God, who is the only one who can rightfully judge our hearts.

Luke 16:15 says "That which is highly esteemed by men (because of appearance) is often an abomination to God."

(Pages 288-299)

Personal Questions

1.   Loving others is only possible if we are **loving God**. (Matthew 22:37; 2 Corinthians 8:5) Then God will enable us to love others **before** or **instead** of ourselves. (2 Corinthians 4:10-12; 1 John 4:12)

2.   Give an example of a situation where you experienced God's Love flowing through you. Did the situation change? Did the other person change? Were you able to continue to love even though you didn't see any changes? (1 Corinthians 13:8; Luke 6:27-28)

See example about God's Love in Chapter 2, "Burnt Roast."

See example about God's Love in Chapter 12, "I Love You More Than the Carpeting." See example about God's Love in Chapter 12, "Did You Tell Him Off?"

3.   Only a person **loving God** can be transparent and admit failures about himself.

(Pages 283-284)

4.   Self-life wants to **hide the truth**, whereas God's Life wants to **expose the truth**.

(Pages 281-282)

5. Are there any key points in this chapter that you are still struggling with?

    Open discussion.

Continue at Home

1. Write on a note card all the Scriptures in this chapter that particularly ministered to you. Use them to help you apply these principles. Memorize them.

2. Ask God to help you become aware of the times you are "consumed with yourself," either arrogantly or in a "self-pity" way. Choose to confess these things, repent of them, and give them over to God. Go through your Inner Court Ritual.

3. If you feel you are not loving others the way God desires, ask Him to show you the areas in your life that are blocking your relationship with Him and preventing His Love from flowing.

4. This week as you learn more about loving others as yourself, ask God to show you further ways you can *agapao* your husband, your children, your parents, your family, your boss, etc. Begin to walk God's Love in your life. Be an *extension of His Love*.

READ:	MEMORIZE:
I John 3 and 4	1 Peter 1:22
John 14,15,17	1 John 4:7-8,12,17,21
1 Corinthians 13	John 15:12-13; 13:34
Philippians 2	1 John 3:18

Chapter 16: Loving in Our Marriages
DVD 4 - Session 8 - 36 minutes

God's Will for our lives

- To unconditionally love (agapao) our spouses, no matter where they are (married, separated, divorced).

- If we are not doing this, we are not loving God first.

We are to love (agapao) unconditionally

- If we have a difficult time with "submission:"

  - We should remember the Second Commandment first.

  - We are to love our spouses whether or not they are believers and whether or not they are returning our Love.

- If we have a difficult time applying the Second Commandment:

  - We should remember God wants us to love (agapao) our enemies with this same kind of Love.

  - The word for love in both of these commandments is agapao—to totally give ourselves over to.

Live Christ's Life

- Not sloppy Agape—love without God's Wisdom.

- God's Love and His Wisdom go together—they are that perfect balance.

- God's Wisdom teaches us how to walk in God's Love wisely.

Chesed Love

- Old Testament word for Love which has two facets:

  - One is a longsuffering Love.

  - One is a discipline Love.

- Which type of love is appropriate to use for our situation? Only God, through the Mind of Christ, can tell us.

Tough love

- With true Agape Love, the people are brought closer to each other—Agape never fails.

- In the flesh, it's easy to be tough—to put up guidelines and consequences.

- If we are not walking by the Spirit, then it's human love and not God's Love at all.

- If we are walking by the Spirit (a cleansed vessel), then it's truly God's Love.

Loving God's Way

- This does not mean overlooking the sin, pretending that it does not exist, or pointing it out and trying to fix it.

- We must first give our feelings about the sin to God, and trust God to do something about it—i.e., get out of the way.

- We don't need to trust our spouses completely in order to love them—we need only to trust God completely (this won't work if it's human love).

God fulfills our basic needs

- It doesn't matter what our marital status is, God is the one who fulfills our two basic needs.

- The "if only's" must stop—we *can* be loved and we *can* love regardless of where we are walking now.

- If we are happily married, it's often harder to look to God to meet these needs.

- Satan is on an all-out attack on marriage and family.

Marriage vows

- Marriage means to fit, join or cleave like glue (bind ourselves to another)—no matter what hap- pens.

- As Christians we have only two rights:

  -    The right to know God's Will.

  -    The right to have His Power to carry it out.

- The Bible is our guideline.

Christian counsel

- Don't seek secular help—you will only receive secular answers.

- There are not just two choices in a troubled marriage—there is a third option (to temporarily separate and seek God).

When God restores a marriage

- It will not be the same as before.

- When Agape becomes the foundation, all human loves will have a chance to be rekindled. Agape can carry a marriage until that time.

- If both partners refuse to initiate God's Love, that marriage will probably fail.

- It only takes one partner to initiate God's Love—and the relationship can change.

No "doormat" feelings

- God will not allow us to be taken advantage of—because we are doing His Will.

- He will be our armor and our protection.

- We will feel more like "powerhouses" because it's God's Life through us, not our own—this is strength, not weakness.

Our responsibility

- Accept that God loves us.

- Love (agapao) God with all our heart, will and soul.

- Love (agapao) our spouse before or instead of ourselves.

God's responsibility

- The Holy Spirit will show us how to love wisely.

- God will change and transform our spouse in His timing and in His way.

- God will work out His Will in our spouse's life.

- We are not responsible for what our spouse thinks or chooses to do, we are just to love (agapao) the "whole package."

Focus on Jesus

- We need to stop strangle holding our mates.

- Stop trying to conform them into our desired image for a mate.

- Trust God to fix what He wants in our mates.

Marriage in God's eyes

- Marriage is a prophetic picture of our relationship with God.

- We need to be willing to love even if our circumstances and situations never change.

Your choice

- Abundant Life—experiencing God's Life in place of our own.

- Joy, Peace and Love come not with absence of trials, but with the presence of Jesus.

Group Discussion Questions

1. Whether we are married, separated, divorced, single, or widowed, what is the most important thing we can do? (1 Peter 4:8; 1 John 3:17-18; 4:7-8,20-21; John 13:35; Romans 13:8)

   The most important thing we can do as Christians, no matter where we are, is to love—to unconditionally love our neighbors as ourselves.

   This is the meaning and purpose of our lives as Christians. If we don't learn to love and be loved the way God intends, we will have wasted our lives.

   (Pages 57-58, 295)

2. If we are not loving with God's Love, what is wrong? (1 John 3:14-15; 4:7-8,20) Why?

   If we are not loving as God desires (others before ourselves), something is wrong with our relation- ship with God and we are not loving Him as we are supposed to. There is obviously something preventing us from being those open channels and we must "deal with" that sin first.

   (Page 295)

   See example in Chapter 14, "Twenty Years of Buried Hurt."

3. In Ephesians 5:22 it says, "Wives, submit yourselves unto your own husbands." If we have a hard time with this principle, what Scripture should we remember to apply first?

   If we are having a hard time with submission to our husbands, we should simply apply the Second Commandment (Matthew 22:39) before Ephesians 5:22. This commandment tells us to agapao (totally give ourselves over to) our husbands before, or instead of, ourselves. In other words, we are to put his will and desires before our own.

   (Pages 295-296)

4. If we still cannot lay our wills and our lives down to our spouses because of "justified hurts," what further Scriptures should we always keep in mind?

   God goes even further, and in Luke 6:27-28, He tells us we are to agapao our enemies with this same kind of Love. Perhaps at certain times some of our husbands would fit into this category.

   (Page 296)

   Romans 12:20-21 tells us the way we overcome evil is with good.

5. Who loved (agapao) us, even when we were still enemies of the cross? (Romans

5:8; 19-21)

Jesus Christ loved us (agapao), even when we were sinners and enemies of the Cross. He chose, even then, to be an open vessel of Love to us. This is our example and what He desires that we all do unto others.

(Pages 296-297)

6.   What is it that teaches us how to love wisely? (Psalm 32:8)

7.   Define "sloppy Agape" or unbalanced love.

Sloppy Agape is God's longsuffering and merciful Love without being balanced by His Wisdom and discernment. It's Love that only knows God's mercy, but not His justice or righteousness. True Agape Love is the perfect balance between God's Mercy and His Righteousness.

(Pages 297-298)

8.   When we encounter someone in our family immersed in sin, in general, what is the best way to handle it? (1 Peter 4:8) Do we point out the sin to them and try to fix it ourselves? (Colossians 3:12-13; Romans 2:4; 12:21)

The best way to handle a family member immersed in sin is not to continually point it out, take responsibility to fix it, or pretend that it doesn't exist, but to give our feelings about the sin to God and then trust Him to do something about it. It's hard to keep our hands off the situation, but it's the only way that works. God will show us what our role in the remedy (if any) should be.

(Pages 304-306)

9.   What are our own three responsibilities in loving our spouses? (Isaiah 43:4a; Matthew 22:37; Matthew 22:39) What are God's responsibilities in our marriages? (James 1:5; Psalm 32;8; Romans 8:28; Isaiah 55:8-9)

Our three responsibilities in loving our spouses are:

1)   Accepting that God loves us.

2)   Loving God with all our heart, will and soul.

3)   God's Love will then be released through us and we'll be enabled to love our spouses unconditionally.

God's three responsibilities are:

1)   The Holy Spirit will show us *how* to love wisely (with the Mind of Christ).

2)   God will change and transform our spouses in His timing and in His way.

3)   God will work out His perfect Will in the way He knows is best.

(Pages 311-312, 316-317)

10. If our spouse asks us to do something ungodly, what should our response be? (Exodus 1:17; Daniel 3 & 6; Acts 5:29)

If our spouse asks us to do something ungodly, then our obedience to God must supersede our loyalty to our spouse and we need to take steps to remedy the situation. We need to seek competent counsel, temporarily separate if God leads us to, and use the time to seek God and His Will.

(Pages 304-305)

11. Think of some Scriptural examples where God's Love and His Wisdom were the complete solution to the problems. (Genesis 37:5-45:8) Are there any circumstances or situations in your life where God's Love can't be the solution? (John 13:35; 1 Corinthians 13:8a)

I love the story of Joseph. How his brothers envied him, threw him in a pit, and sold him to travelers going down to Egypt. Joseph had every right to be angry and seek revenge. But, even after Joseph became Pharaoh's right-hand person and had the opportunity to get back at his brothers, because God was his all consuming passion, God's Love and Wisdom carried him through. And Joseph continued to love his brothers as God would have him to do. In Genesis 45:5, Joseph says (upon seeing his brothers), "Don't be angry with yourselves; it was not you who sent me here, but God." Only God's Love and forgiveness in his life could have brought him to the point where he could mean that with all his heart. God's Love is the solution to all our problems, if we will only let it be.

Personal Questions

1. The definition of marriage is a commitment or a **vow** before the Lord. (Deuteronomy 23:21; Ecclesiastes 5:4) Marriage in God's eyes means to fit, join, and **become one**. (Genesis 2:23-24; 1 Peter 3:8; Philippians 2:2; 1 Corinthians 1:10; Matthew 19:5-6; Ephesians 5:28)

(Pages 307-308)

2. Why did God institute marriage in the first place? (Hosea 2:20)

God instituted marriage as a prophetic picture of our relationship with Him. It's an earthly picture of how wonderful a loving relationship could be—how two people could become one.

(Page 311)

3. In any marriage, God's **Word** and His **Spirit** must always work together. (Ephesians 3:17-19; 4: 15a; Philippians 1:9) Why?

God's Word and His Spirit together are Truth. Jesus is the Word that became, by His Spirit, the Deed. He is the Word that became flesh. God's Word tells us what His Will is and then His Spirit performs it in our lives.

(Page 120)

4. Which type of love (human or divine) best describes your marriage? Explain.

    Open discussion.

5. <u>READ</u>: Genesis 12:11-20 and 1 Peter 3:5-6. Who can we trust to deal with our spouse's sin? Explain. (John 8:3-12; Romans 2:4; 1 Peter 3:1-2; 2 Samuel 7:14; Hebrews 12:5-7) Give Scriptural examples.

    God is the only one we can trust to deal with our spouse's or anyone's sin. We are to obey our spouses but trust God, as Sarah did. So we don't have to trust our spouses completely, only God.

    A good Scriptural example is, again, Joseph. In the situation with his brothers, he didn't take matters into his own hands to punish his brothers, he simply trusted God to deal with his brothers' sin and God did (Genesis 37:5, 45:8).

    (Pages 304-305)

6. Our two basic needs are **to be loved** and **to love**. Is it our spouses' responsibility to meet these two needs for us? Why/Why not? (Philippians 4:19)

    No, it is *not* our spouse's responsibility to meet our two basic needs. Our spouses can never fully satisfy our needs and if we look to them to do so, we'll both sink. If we can look to God for our need "to be loved," then we'll have the proper foundation to lay our wills and lives down so that He might love others through us. And thus, fulfill our second basic need.

    (Pages 29, 57-58, 91-92, 306-307)

7. Are you "living the truth" in your home—do your words and your deeds match? In other words, do your actions inside your home match your words at church? Can your spouse tell that you are a Christian by your actions?

    I pray that our actions at home (most of the time) match our words at church. I pray that we are all learning how to be genuine.

    Being truthful also means being faithful—doing what we say we will do. Galatians 2:20 says we are to live by the faithfulness of God to perform what He promises in His Word. We should also want to be faithful to Him and perform what we promise Him.

    (Pages 120, 276-277)

8. See the *Marriage Relationship* Scriptures in the Supplemental Notes found in the back of the textbook. Put the ones that particularly minister to you on 3x5 cards and memorize them.

    (Pages 347-349)

9. John 10:10 says that God desires us to have *abundant Life* right where we are walking today. Are you experiencing this? Explain.

Open discussion.

Abundant Life does not mean an abundance of blessings or things, but simply experiencing God's Love when you know you have none of your own to give, His Wisdom when you don't know what to do, and His Power when you have no strength.

(Page 313)

10.   The meaning to life lies in our **<u>relationships</u>**. First our **<u>relationship</u>** with God and then our **<u>relationship</u>** with others. (Luke 10:25, 27-28) Joy, peace, and love come not with the absence of **<u>trials</u>**, but only with the presence of **<u>God</u>**. (Psalm 16:11; 1 John 4:7-8)

(Page 322)

Continue for the Rest of Your Life

Don't put this study on a shelf and forget it. Continually keep God's Way of Agape foremost in your mind. Keep reading The Way of Agape textbook and listening to the tapes. Constantly renew your thinking in order to stay an open channel, receiving His Love, and then being a vessel to pass it on.

"If ye, then, be risen with Christ, seek those things which are above, where Christ sitteth on the right hand of God. Set your affection on things above, not on things on the earth. For ye are dead, and your life is hidden with Christ in God. When Christ, *who is our life,* shall appear, then shall ye also appear with Him in glory.

"Mortify, therefore, your members which are upon the earth...put off all these: anger, wrath, malice, blasphemy, filthy communication out of your mouth. Lie not one to another, seeing that ye have put off the old man with his deeds, And have put on the new man, which is renewed in knowledge after the image of Him that created him....*And above all these things put on [Agape], which is the bond of perfectness.*" (Colossians 3:1-5, 8-10, 14)

Conclusion

God is Love and, if we are believers, His Love is "in us" (in our hearts). The only way, however, that His Love can come forth from our hearts out into our lives is if we are open and cleansed vessels. We must constantly choose to set aside, relinquish and die to our own self (our own thoughts, emotions and desires that are contrary to God's) so that God can love His Love through us.

The reason God so often allows trials and tribulations into our lives is so we might learn to unconditionally lay down at His feet all our thoughts, emotions and desires that are contrary to His, justified or not. Then His Love in our hearts will not "grow cold," as Scripture warns, but will freely flow out into all our relationships. And we can "be in this world as He is," and that is *LOVE*!

"Strait is the gate, and narrow is the way, which leadeth unto life, and *few* there be that find it." (Matthew 7:14, emphasis added)

Will you be one that does?

"Blessed be God, even the Father of our Lord Jesus Christ, the Father of mercies, and the God of all comfort; Who comforteth us in all our tribulation, that we may be able to comfort them which are in any trouble, by the comfort wherewith we ourselves are comforted of God."

2 Corinthians 1:3-4